More Fast Ideas for Busy Teachers

100 Productive Activities for Teachers, Substitutes, and Parents

by
Greta Barclay Lipson, Ed.D.

illustrated by Susan Kropa

Cover by Susan Kropa

Good Apple
1204 Buchanan St., Box 299
Carthage, IL 62321-0299

Paramount Publishing

Copyright © Good Apple, 1994

ISBN No. 0-86653-821-6

Printing No. 98765432

Good Apple
1204 Buchanan St., Box 299
Carthage, IL 62321-0299

Table of Contents

GA1513

GA1513

GA1513

GA1513

Introduction

The success of *Fast Ideas for Busy Teachers* (GA1082) was the inspiration for this follow-up book. I have put together a similar compendium in response to enthusiastic teachers and parents who expressed an interest in a sequel.

You will find a plan in this book for every mood, be it quiet, active or in-between. There are exercises for whole class participation, for groups, partnerships, and for solo endeavors. Use these versatile ideas for discussion, creative interpretation, or written expression. The ideas are sound and will yield hearty student response and participation.

This book can be depended upon as a timeless lifesaver and desktop companion for the busy teacher. Some of the suggestions on the following pages are instant winners. Some may need a little time and preparation, but all are workable and have been teacher-tested with real students.

I encourage you to use this book of activities in any way that suits your particular style. Whatever enterprise may be suggested–always execute it your way. You are the best judge of what will work for your class most effectively. Expand an idea, take a portion of it, or use it to seed a more ambitious project. Above all, enhance the material with your own vision.

On a personal note, I want my readers to know that I always enjoy hearing from hard-working teachers and their lively students! I would love receiving class letters, snapshots, teacher responses, and any odds and ends which demonstrate the good use you have made of this book. And for that I thank you very much in advance.

The Three Princes of Serendip

> The word *serendipity* means to make fortunate discoveries quite by accident. In the Persian fairy tale, these important discoveries were made by the acute powers of the Three Princes of Serendip who traveled widely and always uncovered exciting knowledge along the way. This collection of activities extends an invitation to teachers and their students to do the same.

A conscientious teacher has already asked the question, "Can I identify the learning objectives of these activities?" The answer is, "Yes." All the ideas in this book are replete with skills within an arrangement that presents the exercises in fresh and alternative ways.

The objective in *More Fast Ideas for Busy Teachers* is to give students the opportunity to experience language in a spontaneous way using a variety of modes and devices. The material invites a different approach to rhetoric while capitalizing on flexibility, resourceful thinking, and unusual solutions to questions posed. In this constellation of assignments there is strength in serendipity!

Here is an opportunity to play with language in all its versatility. The materials encourage students to innovate, to mold and explore, to be funny and serious. These activities allow the freedom to be venturesome and work the language like yeast dough from which any shape, size, and dimension can emerge. Since we are granted license, let's throw sweet stuff into that wonderful leavened metaphor as an agent of active learning.

English skills are embedded in these creative ideas on many levels—a fact which produces a synergy in working with language. The approach in this book does something different than formal lessons and may even generate more learning because it is solidly in the comfort zone. Within this format reading, writing, and spoken language are not ends in themselves but are tools for communicating ideas and information effectively.

GA1513

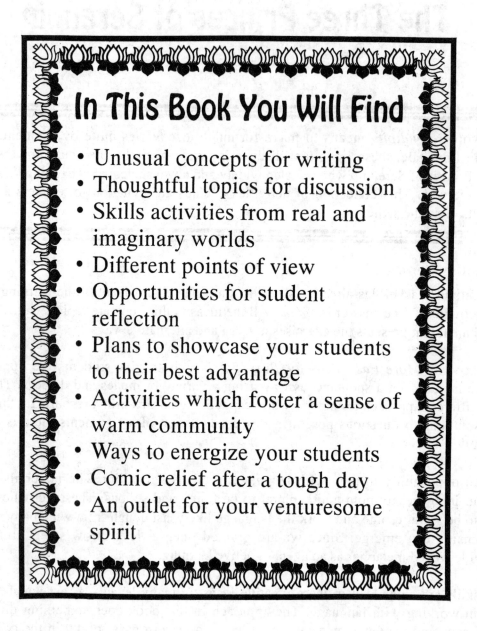

In This Book You Will Find

- Unusual concepts for writing
- Thoughtful topics for discussion
- Skills activities from real and imaginary worlds
- Different points of view
- Opportunities for student reflection
- Plans to showcase your students to their best advantage
- Activities which foster a sense of warm community
- Ways to energize your students
- Comic relief after a tough day
- An outlet for your venturesome spirit

x

GA1513

Ack Endings

Choose one person to call out the following questions to the entire class. The response to each question will be a one-word answer which ends in the letters *ac*, *ack*, or *aque*. Any class member can respond with the answer. Another strategy is to hand out a random list of *ac* or *ack* words to which the students can refer. The same exercise can be a paper and pencil matching assignment. Increase the list by calling for contributions from the students.

Example:

Oral Question	Response
Old farmers magazine	almanac
Something to hold potatoes	sack
Odds and ends for your china cabinet	knickknacks
A reference to your heart	cardiac
An Indian chief	Pontiac
A smart remark	crack
A really expensive car	Cadillac
To make camp in a temporary setting	bivouac
A train travels on it	track
A person who always seems sick	hypochondriac
Someone who has a hard time falling asleep	insomniac
Stuff piled high	stack
A picture in a deck of cards	Jack
The opposite of front	back
Not a nail but a _____	tack
Gunfire from an antiaircraft cannon	flack
A film company	Kodak
A wild, long-haired ox	yak
A person who cuts down trees	lumberjack
Another word for pancake	flapjack
An Eskimo canoe	kayak
A film on your teeth	plaque

1

Address Syllables

Consider your address as a pattern of syllables that suggests a form for a phrase, a remark, or a reflective statement which makes good sense. It works like this: First write your address horizontally with the street name. Then write it vertically. Each numeral indicates the number of syllables for that line. Zero allows for a sentence of any length. When you are finished, add an author's name by taking the street name as a surname and adding a given name that makes a good fit. That will be your new nom de plume (pen name). You may also use your ZIP codes for longer phrases!

12740 Carlos

1	Well!
2	Hi there.
7	I've seen you around town, kid.
4	You seem okay.
0	Could we talk sometime?

by Juan Carlos

544 Rodrigues

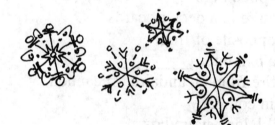

5	I would give the world
4	To see the snow
4	Melt into spring.

by Rosetta Rodrigues

15343 Palmerston

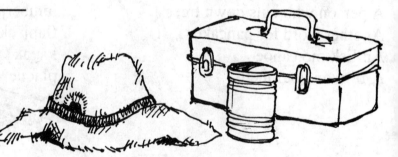

1	Grab
5	That fishing tackle
3	Bring those worms
4	Your old straw hat
3	And let's fish!

by Monica Palmerston

GA1513

Applause! Applause!

There are some small things that we can do to make friends and acquaintances feel good about themselves if we only remember how little it takes to pat someone on the back! It doesn't cost a cent to extend a kind word or give a compliment, but it is worth a great deal to the recipient! One technique to use in the classroom to acknowledge another person's value seems funny at first, but it works and leaves people with a glow!

To develop a warm sense of community, conduct an "Applause, Applause" session once a week. Invite a few volunteers to stand in front of the class and, one at a time, tell something they recently did for themselves or another person that was really nice or sensible or satisfying. Maybe they cleaned their rooms without being nagged, took their siblings to a Saturday movie, or took the garbage to the curb without being asked.

The teacher may choose to lead off the event with some satisfying declaration of his or her own. Perhaps she or he corrected students' papers on Friday immediately after school and had a great, free weekend for a change. When the presenter finishes, everyone in class stands and applauds vigorously! That person chooses another person to stand and once again the presenter enjoys a moment of celebrity!

3

GA1513

Arcane Words

We do not know the meanings of many of the words we encounter in our reading, but some of those words are fascinating because they have a wonderfully curious quality. Even though we may be wrong, we sometimes take a chance at a wild definition that sounds like it could fit! And that is the point of this game.

Look at the list of strange words below. (If the class develops its own list, it must include words no one knows!) Select five or more words and then supply your own made-up definitions. In the spirit of fun, use the words in a sentence. Read the made-up definitions and sentences aloud. Which sound the most reasonable or entertaining?

After this preliminary work, consult the dictionary to find the real meanings. As a follow-up, keep a class list of strange words for a similar exercise. Is the word *arcane* a mystery to you?

arcane: (adjective) mysterious
curmudgeon: (noun) a bad-tempered person
debacle: (noun) a sudden, disastrous defeat or downfall
egregious: (adjective) conspicuously bad or offensive
garbology: (noun) the scientific study of a society's garbage
gargoyle: (noun) a roof spout in the form of a monster
lollygag: (verb) dawdle, to waste time by puttering around
lugubrious: (adjective) mournful, gloomy, dismal
mawkish: (adjective) excessively sentimental
miasma: (noun) a noxious gas
obsequious: (adjective) exhibiting fawning behavior
phlegmatic: (adjective) having a calm temperament
pochard: (noun) a species of a diving duck
rutabaga: (noun) a thick root used as food
widget :   (noun) an unnamed mechanical gadget
quixotic: (adjective) caught up in romantic ideals and unreachable goals

WIDGET?

VIDEO ARCANE

OIL

LUGUBRIOUS ?

4

Associated Ideas

This can be a whole class "call out" exercise which involves associated ideas and vocabulary development. Students may suggest four categories of main headings which are listed on the chalkboard. Related words, phrases, or clauses are called out to be written in their respective categories. Proceed one category at a time. Establish a comfortable time limit before moving on to the next category. If someone suggests words or phrases that seem unrelated, these suggestions must be defended. Consider *clothes*, *Hollywood*, *outer space*, or *cars*.

Example:

Music

Pop
Rhythm and Blues
Rock
Country
Classical
Folk
Big Band
Jazz
Reggae

It would be helpful to have two recording assistants to keep a written list which can be duplicated or kept as a continuing record of the activity.

Backward Rhymes

There are two ways of writing and reading backward rhymes. The variations are quite diverse. When you bring creativity to the task and mix the backward words with frontward words, your sense of humor does the rest.

Mother Goose rhymes can help in this enterprise because many of them are silly from the start! Pick a rhyme that is short and sweet and try it both ways. A demonstration on the chalkboard with the entire class would help. This activity is a challenge which creates a strangely wild experience.

Directions:

1. The first method is to write from left to right just as an English reader and speaker would. You may reverse all the words or just a few for the weirdest effect.
2. The second method is to start from right to left and work things out in that fashion.

STYLE 1.   LEFT TO RIGHT WITH A FEW RECOGNIZABLE WORDS
      Rebrab, rebrab, shave a gip,
      Woh many sriah will make a giw?
      Ruof and ytnewt, that's enough
      Give the rebrab a pinch of ffuns.

STYLE 2.   FROM RIGHT TO LEFT WITH
NO RECOGNIZABLE WORDS

      Gip a evahs, rebrab, rebrab
      Giw a ekam lliw sriah ynam woh
      Hguone staht, ytnewt dna ruof
      Ffuns fo hcnip a rebrab eht evig

      Ti yrt uoy won

Solution: Barber, barber, shave a pig,
              How many hairs will make a wig?
              Four and twenty, that's enough.
              Give the barber a pinch of snuff.

GA1513

Basketball Is Born*

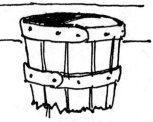

Basketball was invented in the U.S. in 1891 by James Naismith, a gym teacher, who was employed at the YMCA Training School in Springfield, Massachusetts. His department head asked him to create a game that could be played indoors or out. Naismith proceeded to work out a team sport with eighteen men on a team because that was exactly the number of students enrolled in his class!

In order to play the game he needed two baskets suspended from the balcony of the gym. When the janitor attached two half-bushel baskets (used for peaches), they worked so well that his innovation became the basis for the name of the sport. Everything about the game was so fascinating to sports enthusiasts that news of it circulated wildly throughout the U.S. and Canada.

Basketball has evolved in the past one hundred years, but it is still flexible enough to be played by teams, with just a couple of participants, or one person playing solo. The most significant change in the game affected the basket. In the early stages of basketball, every time a player made a basket the ball would get stuck in the basket and would have to be freed by someone on a ladder. The backboard of the basket was added to eliminate audience interference, and finally the rim of the basket was changed to metal.

It is hard to believe that this sport–dreamed up by a teacher in response to his boss's request–would grow to become the most highly attended sport in the country. Basketball fans are numbered literally in the millions. It is played in schools, colleges, professional arenas, side drives, back alleys, and in any place where a basket can be attached to a support.

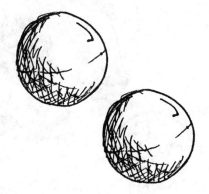

---

* *A Book for All Seasons*, (GA1153) by Greta B. Lipson, Good Apple, Inc., copyright 1990, Carthage, Illinois.

GA1513

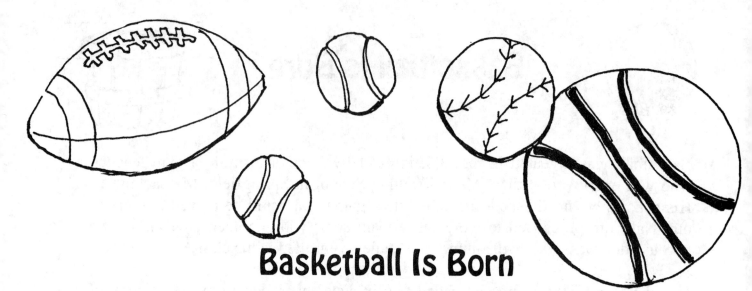

Basketball Is Born

- If you were required to make up a game, could you meet the challenge? Try it, name it, and be able to explain it to the class.

- Describe a basketball, baseball, or football game you attended where the sportsmanship and the stunning performance filled the crowd with terrific pride and enthusiasm. What occurred at the game?

- Have you ever been frightened by the behavior of the crowd at a school game? What are your comments about this occurrence? Do you have any recommendations to make to the school administration about the conduct in general regarding school sports?

- Watch the sports section of your daily newspaper for an exciting account of a spectator sport. Cut it out and bring it to school for a class sports collection.

- For rare sports poetry read "The Base Stealer" by Robert Francis and "Foul Shot" by Edwin A. Hoey in the collection, *Reflections on a Gift of Watermelon Pickle & Other Modern Verse*, edited by Stephen Dunning, Lothrop, Lee & Shepard Books, 1966. Search for more sports poetry. It does exist!

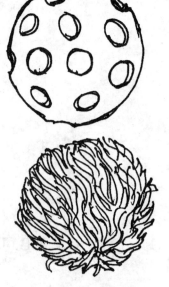

Brainology

Do you know about stupology?
Or the star who loves beautology
Do you know a guy with ego-ology
Or a dog who studies barkology
Or our baby who does cryology
Or a pilot who knows flyology
Or a kid whose career is smartology
Or the sneak who practices smarmology
Have you seen the tough who takes muscleology
Or the chef who thrives on cookology
Or the ratty kid who does rottenology
Or the fat kid who understands eatology
Or the dad who majors in nagology
Or the sport who's freaked with jockology
Or the teacher who's an expert in bore-ology
Or the big mouth who suffers from mouthology
Or the liar who practices fibology
Or my kid brother who was born with pestology
Or the flea brain who studies bubbleology
Or the big shot who is expert at bullology?

Greta B. Lipson

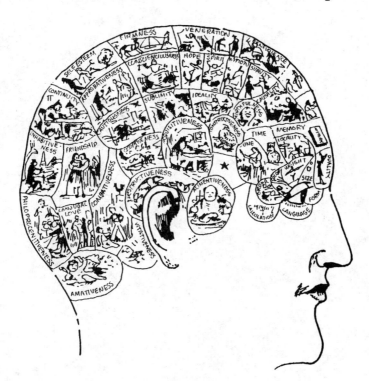

GA1513

Brainology

- Create an ongoing, alphabetical class list of authentic "ologys." Develop another list of made-up "ologys." Students may add contributions in magic marker. Watch the list grow!

anthropology
archaeology
astrology
audiology
biology
chronology
craniology
ecology
entomology
eschatology
etymology
garbology
gemology
genealogy
geology
histology
immunology
meteorology
microbiology
neology
neurology
oncology
otolaryngology
pathology
pharmacology
phrenology
physiology
psychology
sarcology
scatology
sociology
tautology
technology
theology
urbanology
urology

GA1513

Certificate of Honor

If you have ever wished that you could show your appreciation or admiration for someone but didn't quite know how to express it, here is a great opportunity to reveal your feelings! It can work for every occasion and for any person: a grandparent, a parent, an important adult in your life, a teacher, a coach, a brother or sister, a wonderful friend, relatives of all ages, a crossing guard, a club sponsor, a mail carrier, a librarian, the school secretary. The list is endless and all you have to do is duplicate the following award. Use your best handwriting or printing. Hand it to that special person in your life and "SHAZAM"–you have magically said "Thank You" and have truly made someone feel wonderful!

GA1513

Award Certificate

Name of Honoree_____

       is hereby honored and acknowledged as an outstanding person

for _____

_____

      in the City and State of_____

Respect and the highest regard will be accorded the recipient of this award in keeping with all standards of celebrity.

_____
Signed with Profound Appreciation

_____On This Date

Official Seal

GA1513

Chow Down

Judi Barrett wrote an outrageous story entitled *Cloudy with a Chance of Meatballs*, Macmillan Children's Book Group, 1978. The story is set in the town of "Chewandswallow" where the menu comes rolling in as part of the weather three times a day. All the edibles come magically from the sky. There are hamburger storms, beans blown in by the wind, and lemon gelatin molds seen setting in the west. It is often a hazardous place to live, with mashed potatoes plopping on people's heads and cherry pie whizzing by. But the daily menu is always a great gastronomic surprise! Can you describe some of the problems these people must have? Can you visualize or illustrate some of the food weather that comes over the town of Chewandswallow?

Try to track down this bizarre story with its zany illustrations to get into the food mood. An additional assignment is to make a trip to the library as a book sleuth. Try to locate and record as many titles as you can that have some kind of food in the title (for a good reference guide, be sure to include the authors). Put a star next to some of the books you would like to read and review for the class. A few of these intriguing books are:

- *My Darling, My Hamburger* by Paul Zindel
- *The Chocolate War* by Robert Cormier
- *Me and the Eggman* by Eleanor Clymer
- *A Hero Ain't Nothin' but a Sandwich* by Alice Childress
- *Reflections on a Gift of Watermelon Pickle* by S. Dunning
- *You Can't Eat Peanuts in Church and Other Little Known Laws* by Barbara Seuling
- *Soupsongs* by Ray Blount, Jr.
- *The Carp in the Bathtub* by Barbara Cohen
- *Smashed Potatoes* edited by Jane G. Martel

Chuckle Poem

Some words have rhyming possibilities that go on and on in an endless stream. Consider the word *cat* and you know what we mean. If you list some words and phrases that rhyme with *cat* and you add to that collection the wonderful ingredient of humor, you have the beginnings of something we call a *chuckle poem*. Here are some ideas to string together in any way you like. Add your own rhyming words to it and your own rhyme scheme. Make sure your poem makes sense, and then you've got it!

My Pets

Bad dog and cat
The dog's named Pat
And he's quite fat
The other is Scat
He's our thin cat
Sleeps on a mat
They had a spat
Pat knocked Scat flat
Oh drat!

What are some words that come to mind which have multiple rhyme possibilities that can be used for other chuckle poems? Consider *fly, high, sky, pie, try, oh my.* Consider *red, fled, lead, sped, bed, bread, said, dead.* Consider *jar* and *band.*

Clichés

An expression or a phrase which you hear over and over again in common usage is called a cliché. Clichés are found in print and heard in the spoken word all the time. These worn-out phrases may seem handy, but they become tiresome and lose their impact because they are overused. It is tempting to say that something is "flat as a pancake" or "neat as a pin," but it is always more effective if you write or speak about a topic with your own impressions and in your own words. As a class try restating the following clichés orally or in writing. You do not have to create figures of speech. Simply be straightforward in your phrases or sentences. Add your own tired clichés to this list of old-timers.

Say These in Your Own Way:

Old as the hills
Big as a house
Fresh as a daisy
Light as a feather
At the crack of dawn
Pretty as a picture
Beauty is only skin deep.
My heart was in my mouth.
I could eat a horse.
Sweet as sugar
They moved lock, stock and barrel.
His head is in the clouds.
Proud as a peacock
White as snow
Squeaky clean

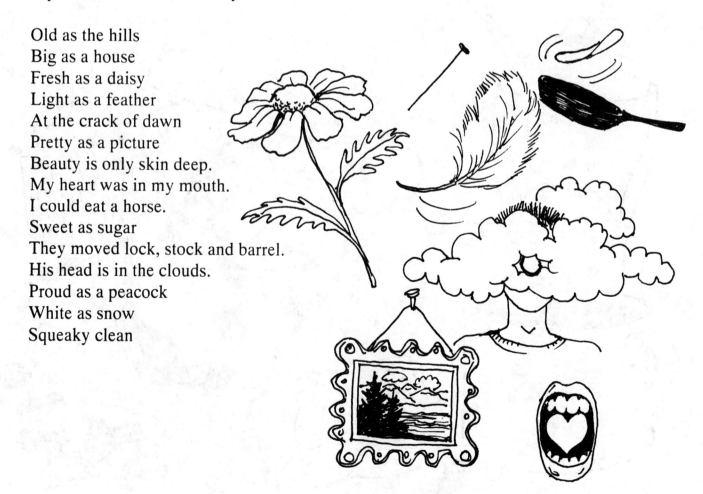

GA1513

Comfort Food

Many people have a "comfort food" which they eat when they are in need of emotional support. It may be something that dates back to when you were very young and had to stay in bed because you were really sick. Or it could be a particular food that you yearn for when you are feeling sad or have the blahs. But it is true that everybody understands this very special need.

Sometimes people put signs on their refrigerators that give a clue to this special soothing food such as the one that says, "Help! Help! I'm in desperate trouble. Send lots of chocolate immediately!" For some people a comfort food may be a nice, hot cup of cocoa with a marshmallow bobbing around. For others it may be chicken noodle soup or potato pancakes or oatmeal cookies. Describe your comfort food on one page with a heartfelt title. What is it? What does it do for you? What circumstances lead up to your need for this food, other than hunger?

GA1513

Create a Tableau

A tableau is a living picture or a frozen scene of an incident that has a message. It is often a grouping of people, in costume, which has dramatic impact. The Nativity is a tableau; the picture of the United States Marines raising the American flag on Iwo Jima is a tableau. All of these creations need not be serious, however. Remember, also, that there is no observable movement taking place–the movement is implied in the eye of the beholder. Working in a group or groups, develop the scenario for a classroom tableau which will have elements in it that are identifiable.

Present the tableau to the class with some costuming to give them a clue. How would the class interpret the message your group was trying to convey? What descriptive words can be used to capture the mood of your tableau? Does it suggest anger, inspiration, conflict, approval, love, confusion, or what?

Following the presentation, ask the class to interpret what they have seen. One troupe member may write the title of the skit on the chalkboard while the others explain the topic of their tableau. Some suggestions for scenes may be:

- An umpire calls a player out while the fuming manager is standing by with other players. Props may be a baseball, hats, a bat.
- The school principal is giving out an award to the biggest brain in the school. The beaming audience of parents is looking on. Props may be books, grown-up apparel, oversized spectacles, and a plaque.
- Parents are driving in the family car while the kids in the back seat are occupied with fighting, playing, eating, entertaining the baby, and being obnoxious.

Daily Schedule

Like busy people everywhere, you are occupied all day long with school, after-school clubs, appointments, homework, volunteer activities, chores, friends, and baby-sitting! The folks in your household have agreed that it would be a good idea if each family member would fill in a weekly schedule so that there would be some idea of where everybody is throughout the day and when to be expected home.

It is not a perfect plan because unexpected things do come up, but soon everyone, children and adults alike, has come to depend upon this practical arrangement. Work out a class schedule for days of the week including after-school plans. Arrange spacing for days, times, and activities for easy reading.

Better yet, you may want to develop a "Weekend Wishful Thinking Fun-Time Schedule" of things you would like to do if you had the money and your wishes could be granted! Enhance the schedule with some attractive artistry.

	MONDAY	TUESDAY	WEDNESDAY	THURSDAY	FRIDAY
6:45	GET UP •	SHOWER •	EAT BREAKFAST ————————————————→		
7:30	MARCHING BAND PRACTICE ——————————————————→				
8:30–4:00	CLASSES ————————————————————————————→				
4:00	CROSS COUNTRY PRACTICE	C.C. MEET	PRACTICE	MEET	PRACTICE
6:00	SUPPER	↓	SUPPER	↓	SUPPER
7:00	PLAY PRACTICE	———→	BELL CHOIR	PLAY PRACTICE	GAME
8:00	↓	↓	HOMEWORK	↓	↓
9:00	TV / HOMEWORK	HOMEWORK	RELAX	HOMEWORK	↓
10:00	BED ————————————————————————→				OUT FOR PIZZA

GA1513

Dear Character

Once in a while you discover a strong character in a story who is so believable that you sincerely wish that person was alive and could be your friend in real life.

Perhaps you have also encountered a character in a book who is a total fool and needs to be straightened out. You are so annoyed by him or her that you would like to offer the benefit of your advice!

Interestingly, some successful authors of young adult literature have recounted touching moments when readers have written letters or called on the phone in search of that very special fictitious character they had come to know well in a story. Most often the young readers had the strong impulse to reach out for help because of strong personal needs.

In either case, if you were given the opportunity to speak face-to-face with any storybook character, what would you say in the way of advice or friendship? Name the story, the character, and the author of the book. Include some background information.

19

Demonstration

A demonstration speech can be informative, entertaining and sometimes, if you're lucky, it can be very funny. Students who have a hobby often welcome the opportunity to share their interests. Think hard about something that you enjoy or a subject which would lend itself to a demonstration speech. Don't be afraid if the topic is as commonplace as "How to Wash a Car." Using all kinds of props is an effective way of making your topic come alive. Envision yourself in front of an audience with a plastic apron, plenty of rags, a bucket, soap, and a microphone.

Select the subject of your speech thoughtfully. Write down the topic with a brief description and hand it in to the teacher. All presentations will be informal but you may want to have a few notes to help you along. Practice at home in front of a mirror. An excellent rehearsal technique is to speak into a tape recorder and then listen to your own delivery. The length of time for all demonstration speeches should be established with the class. The time limit is to be observed by everyone. And remember that shorter is better. How about five minutes?

If this demonstration project gets everyone fired up, your class may want to name its own production company, locate a home video camera, and produce a piece of polished entertainment good enough to show to parents or other classes in the school. The sky is the limit!

Suggested Topics:

1. Clean your room.
2. Make a pizza.
3. Break up a fight.
4. Gift wrap a large package.
5. Eat a four-decker sandwich.
6. Make a model airplane.
7. Pack a lunch.
8. Wash a car.
9. Take a phone message.
10. Order a take-out meal.
11. Apply clown makeup.
12. Teach a dance step.

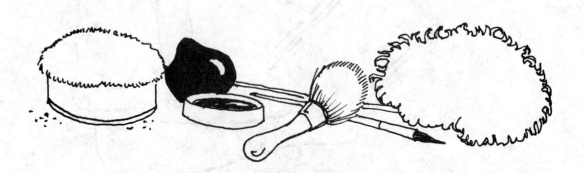

GA1513

Design a T-Shirt

It is about time that people said something positive about students in school who are not great athletes or incredible beauties or Mr./Ms. Popularity! Plain, ordinary, good-hearted people should be accorded some proper recognition!

Assume that you are in the T-shirt business. A bunch of friends from Anytown High come to you and propose that you design some T-shirts celebrating a variety of valuable personal qualities. You agree to the assignment and ask them to produce the ideas for the T-shirts. What would these ideas look like? Have you considered a huge ear for a good listener with an appropriate phrase underneath, a picture of a patient classmate with a halo overhead . . . ? List admirable qualities that should be honored and make suggestions for illustrations. Don't be afraid of abstract graphics and do consult the art teacher.

In the spirit of your class it is also possible to develop a shirt that celebrates a special pride or distinction of your class. This too can be captured in a T-shirt design. A drama group in one school raised money for shirts which read: "The roar of the greasepaint–The smell of the crowd."

GA1513

Dialogue Clues

For starters, try to write a brief snippet of dialogue which you believe is just enough to reveal the personality of a particular character in a scene of your own invention. Use as many or as few sentences as necessary to establish some feeling in the mind of the reader about the person who is speaking.

Example:

"I've got news for you. The world doesn't stop 'cause you're feeling rotten."

One of the techniques a writer has to master is to establish the personality of a character without saying directly to the reader, "Hey this guy Jason is a sneak," or "Marcy is a true hero," or "Charlie is strange but harmless." The author must be able to create dialogue and develop other clues which give a sense of character to the reader. Put yourself into the mind of a writer who tries to reveal the personality of someone.

Here is a way of testing the technique: Choose a small group of people to read some prepared dialogue. Choose another group as listeners. Give the listeners a list of personality types to help them identify the character of the speakers. What other clues from the author helped in your decision?

GA1513

Dialogue

1. "Sorry, but I can't help on the committee. The time is all wrong and meetings will make me late for the beauty parlor every week. You'd better find someone who has more free time." She studied herself closely in her pocket mirror, applied fresh lip gloss and walked out, bouncing her red curls in tune with her jangling bracelets.

2. "So what if there is a designated driver? What's it to me? I'm not a beginning driver, Buster. It won't make any difference because I'm always in control–no matter what." His eyes invited a dare as he lifted the glass to his lips.

3. She ran her hands through her hair and seemed slightly uncomfortable. "Look," she said, "I don't want to embarrass you but I might be able to help you with those problems." She hesitated and then added, "I had a rotten time with the same stuff last term so I know what it's like."

4. "Well, let's see," he said slowly, looking at the ceiling. "It was probably on a Monday. No, I think it was a Tuesday when it started to rain like this because I didn't have an umbrella and–no, wait. It probably was Monday because that's when I forgot to wear my green socks." He droned on endlessly until I wished a flood would come and wash us both away for good.

5. "I know you've tried over and over again with no success," she said, "But hey! Tomorrow is another sunny day and another chance to strut your stuff." She gave me the thumbs-up sign and flashed a million dollar smile.

Listener's Choice:

Identify the speaker who was egotistical, snobbish, greedy, optimistic, boring, clever, dangerous, confused, or helpful. Support your choice. How would you change the dialogue for a clearer impression?

GA1513

Distilled Feelings

In the making of fine wine there is a process of distillation which involves pressing the flavorful juice and the fragrance out of ripe grapes. In much the same way some important ideas in life can be distilled and pressed into a few carefully chosen words.

Sorting through some themes in life, select one (or more) of these subjects that is important to you. Choose a topic that you respond to enthusiastically or deeply. Like compressing aromatic fruit into wine, try to press the essence and the meaning of your chosen theme into sentences or phrases which capture your emotions.

String these reflections together and you have a list of distilled feelings. Start with a strong opening statement that opens up your thoughts. Put a twist on the sentence pattern in any way you wish!

Suggested Topics:
- Music affects body and soul.
- Laughter is a dose of sugar.
- Friends make life worthwhile.
- Reading is total escape.
- Nobody loves you like your dog.

School

School can be different things to different people.
School can be heaven.
School can be the pits.
School can be a place you are forced to be.
School can be a safe haven.
School can be a place where you are nobody.
School can be a place where you shine.
School can be a treasury of friends.
School can be a place where you can grow.

GA1513

Don't Holler—Choral Speaking

The following poem offers many opportunities for effective choral speaking whether or not you have had experience with such a group performance. You may want to consult your music teacher with this venture, but first try out the possibilities with the class, while being open to all suggestions.

An important part of this plan is that everyone must have a copy of the poem so that it can be read like a script as all parts are recited. For the best effect and the most dramatic voices, have the entire class stand to participate. Use solo voices for some parts. Use high voices and low voices. Use different inflections (change in pitch or volume), vary the speed, use the entire group as a chorus for some lines, and work out consistent patterns.

You may want to whisper the line "Don't Holler" and shout it out as the very last line. It is a guaranteed warm and funny experience for everyone.

GA1513

Don't Holler*

I may do dumb things but I'm honest and true
So this is a favor I'm asking of you–
Whatever you do–**Don't Holler!**

My guilt is enough, so don't make it tough
Reproach me and ground me–instruct me and hound me,
But whatever you do–**Don't Holler!**

Keep me inside. Deprive me of air
Threaten and scare me
Mess up my hair
However you punish, I'll consider it fair
But whatever you do–**Don't Holler!**

I'll polish the car and wax all the doors
Shine up the windows and scrub all the floors
I'll attend to the garbage–take it out every week
You won't hear from me–no, nary a peep

I'll sit with the kids, the dog and the cat
I'll never act big or sound like a rat
But whatever you do–**Don't Holler!**

Tell me to stop being mean and sarcastic
I'll get pious and sweet–It'll just be fantastic
No one denies that I did a dumb thing, I'll reform and repent
It won't cost you a cent

Do all of the things, psychologically sound
And sooner or later I'll come around
There are good ways and bad ways to castigate
But there is one way that I earnestly hate.
So–whatever you do–**Don't Holler!**

Remember the punishment should fit the crime
And that's the best way to finish this rhyme.

Greta B. Lipson

* *Audacious Poetry* (GA1417), by Greta B. Lipson, © 1992, Good Apple,
Carthage, Illinois.

Draw a Map

Examine a map of your state or province. Observe carefully all the information which is included such as lines, words, symbols, colors, and legends. Imagine that you are a professional cartographer who draws maps for a living. You have been commissioned to draw a map of the "State of Disarray." It is a strange uncharted place where few have traveled.

It is your job to select the names for villages, rivers, mountains, valleys, forests, and other geographic features. You are sometimes serious and sometimes funny. You may want to place the town of Seepage Drain, Lower Slobovia, or Whoositz Straits. Perhaps you discovered Lachrymose Lake, Slippery Creek, or One-Eyed Gulch. Remember to indicate north, south, east, and west. Include highways, byways, and other routes for travel. Take your time to develop a truly colorful and fascinating map. If it helps, you may choose to use the outline of your own state.

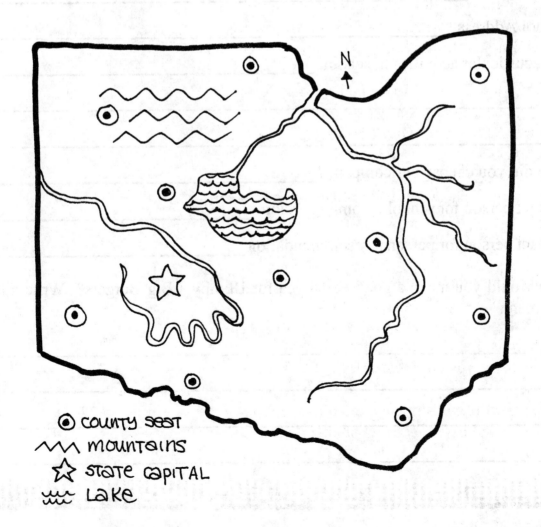

Employment Form

Blimpy's Big Burgers

Employment Application   Date_____

Full-time ☐ Part-time ☐ Days Available: _____

Name _____
             last   first   middle

Address _____
             street   city   state   ZIP

Social Security Number _____

School Name _____

School Address _____

Extracurricular activities in school: _____

_____

_____

Why did you choose our company?_____

Contact person for school recommendation _____

Contact person for personal recommendation _____

Why would you make a good employee for Blimpy's Big Burgers? Write a brief
statement.

_____

_____

_____

_____

Euphemisms

There are some words or phrases or ideas which are so uncomfortable for us to say directly that we find other ways of expressing them. The substitutes we use are called euphemisms, which are expressions that replace the disagreeable words. We don't like to say that someone has died. Instead we use any number of ways to describe death. We say a person passed away, went to his greater reward, kicked the bucket or met his maker, went to heaven, is deceased, and on and on. In *A Dictionary of Euphemisms & Other Doubletalk*, the author Hugh Rawson calls euphemisms "roundabout words."

One of the many funny stories about euphemisms involves the great American circus man P.T. Barnum who was having overcrowding problems in his busy American Museum. His customers were having such a good time they were not leaving at the exit door! His solution was to put up a sign that said "Egress." Since no one knew what it meant, they followed it expectantly only to find they had exited to the outside!

Some Euphemisms	Which Mean
He has a hearty appetite.	He eats like a pig.
I am thrifty.	I'm cheap.
That's a previously owned car.	It's a used car.
You are a creative dresser!	You look like a slob.
They are underprivileged.	They are poor.
Don't expectorate!	Don't spit.
I'm a sanitation engineer.	I am a garbageman.
The kid has a wild imagination.	That kid is a liar.
We have a personality conflict.	We hate each other.

Now you think of some everyday euphemisms you use or have heard.

_____
* For more information about euphemisms in public life, see the publication of the National Council of Teachers of English–Committee on Public Doublespeak, 1111 Kenyon Rd., Urbana, Illinois 61801.

GA1513

Fads and Fashions*

A fad is a fashion that seems to spring up out of nowhere. It catches on quickly. Many people are attracted to it and adopt it enthusiastically. Almost as fast as a fad appears, its attractiveness is exhausted and the style disappears. The topic of fashion generates a lot of heat among parents and young people alike since they do not agree on what styles are appropriate or what is unacceptable. As a good researcher, try to arrive at some answers for the following questions:

- Are students conformists or nonconformists in matters of fashion? Argue for both points of view.
- "Sloppy dressers have sloppy minds!" Is that true? Write a letter to the editor, expressing both pro and con attitudes.
- What is the ugliest fad the adults in your family can remember and describe from their student years?
- What is the ugliest fad that you can remember?
- Make up a fad for male, female, or unisex wear.
- If the class is courageous enough, organize a fashion show with a prize for "The Best in Ugliness."

* *Audacious Poetry* (GA1417), by Greta B. Lipson, © 1992, Good Apple, Carthage, Illinois.

GA1513

Farmer's Problem

Listen to this story and work out a solution. It will help if you diagram the problem on the board.

A farmer had to deliver three things to the town of Boondoggle which was situated across Lake Okeefenokee. He went straightaway to the local boat livery.

"I need your services today as soon as you have a boat available," the farmer said.

The boatman replied, "Before you tell me what you want carried over, I must inform you that I have only a small rowboat for hire today and I can take only one passenger at a time. If you want to get to Boondoggle today, tell me who is going."

The farmer, slightly upset with this information, scratched his head and said, "I have a coyote to deliver to the zoo, a lamb to deliver to the market, and a huge basket of carrots for the cook in the king's castle! I expected to take all three over to the Okeefenokee shore at one time."

"So. What's your problem?" asked the boatman.

"Well," said the farmer, "We can't leave the coyote alone with the lamb because the coyote will eat the wee creature. We can't leave the carrots with the lamb because she'll eat all the carrots! The farmer looked hopefully at the boatman and added, "I have to leave now, but I want to know exactly how you propose to work alone. How will you get all three across in three separate trips and still protect the whole caboodle?"

Solution:

The boatman took the lamb across the lake and left it on the Boondoggle shore. He rowed back, picked up the carrots and took them to the Boondoggle shore, but he took the lamb back with him. He then picked up the coyote to take him to Boondoggle but he left the lamb behind. The boatman made his last trip to pick up the lamb and take him safely to Boondoggle.

GA1513

Fast Transit

You're on a highway traveling north. This morning the weather looked perfect for your long trip, but soon the sky clouded over and now the rain is coming down in buckets. You turn on your headlights because it is overcast so badly it begins to look like dusk. You just hope the other drivers put their lights on too. The windshield wiper is a heavy-duty brand and it's working at max speed. Pretty soon the cars are kicking up an oily film from the road, and you can't keep the windshield clean at all. The temperature takes a nose-dive and the snow starts falling. It's rotten traveling all the way!

We all realize that as advanced as we are in this modern age, we are still at the mercy of the weather. But, there is always the hope that in the city of the future all of that will change.

What will the transportation system look like in the city of the future? Perhaps there will be a gigantic overarching bubble that shields the community from the elements. Discuss the changes in travel and the technological methods of protection from the weather. Illustrate a futuristic city. Include any incredible innovations that occur to you.

GA1513

First Impression

You have always avoided Robin because of an immediate negative response you had to her the first time she walked into class. Months later you were in the public library, working on an assignment, when your stomach told you it was time for a break.

You checked out your books and headed for the door, anxious to get out into the sunshine, when you and Robin collided in the vestibule. Books went helter-skelter and the laughter was spontaneous. Without hesitation, both of you picked up all the scattered stuff that had dropped and you left the building together.

You began to stroll down the library path with Robin at a leisurely pace. You walked through Birmingham Park, talking all the while, and arrived at the refreshment stand–a welcome sight at lunchtime. The two of you decided to buy a hot dog and a drink and sit on the grass, picnic style.

You continued to discuss things through the entire afternoon. As one subject led to another you found yourself talking to Robin as if she were an old friend! She seemed interesting and smart with a rare sense of humor. Best of all she was an attentive listener who didn't interrupt all the time. After a long while, when you both said good-bye, you realized that this had been one of the very best Saturday afternoons you had experienced in a very long time.

But what about your first impression of Robin that had made you avoid her since the beginning of school? Write a paragraph explaining the things about her that had made you wary or uncomfortable. Why did you feel as you did?

In what ways can a first impression be distorted? In your memory, have you ever been completely mistaken about a person after a brief encounter? Discuss superficial things that could lead you to an unfair perception of someone.

GA1513

Fisherman's Talk*

The following is an afternoon encounter in two parts. This face-to-face conversation is from *Inport*, a publication from the Port of Seattle where people come to fish and enjoy casual small talk. Each student in class will be given a copy of this dialogue (without the translation) in order to follow the exchange between the fishermen. Ask for two volunteers to read these parts. Joe talks first and Sam responds.

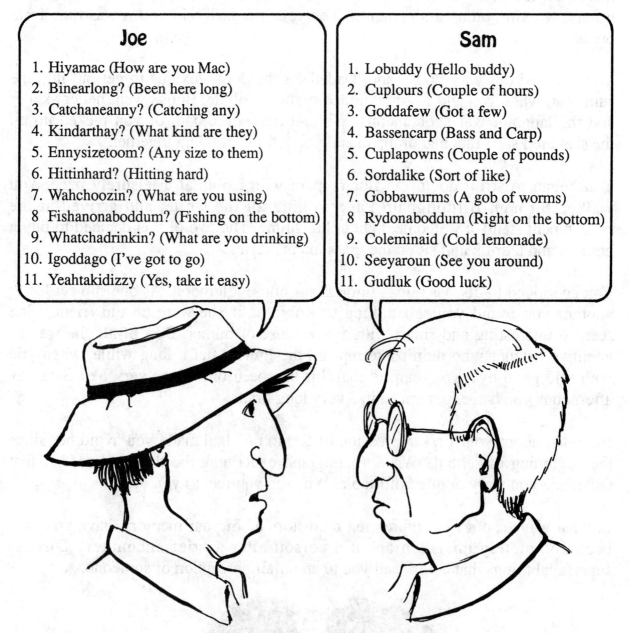

Joe

1. Hiyamac (How are you Mac)
2. Binearlong? (Been here long)
3. Catchaneanny? (Catching any)
4. Kindarthay? (What kind are they)
5. Ennysizetoom? (Any size to them)
6. Hittinhard? (Hitting hard)
7. Wahchoozin? (What are you using)
8 Fishanonaboddum? (Fishing on the bottom)
9. Whatchadrinkin? (What are you drinking)
10. Igoddago (I've got to go)
11. Yeahtakidizzy (Yes, take it easy)

Sam

1. Lobuddy (Hello buddy)
2. Cuplours (Couple of hours)
3. Goddafew (Got a few)
4. Bassencarp (Bass and Carp)
5. Cuplapowns (Couple of pounds)
6. Sordalike (Sort of like)
7. Gobbawurms (A gob of worms)
8 Rydonaboddum (Right on the bottom)
9. Coleminaid (Cold lemonade)
10. Seeyaroun (See you around)
11. Gudluk (Good luck)

Try this difficult trick of writing phrases with an inner ear attuned to the slurred sounds we actually use in conversation. Wujasay?

---

* Anonymous from *Inport*, a publication of the Port of Seattle, port communications office. Rick Winkelman, Staff Assistant, said, "Use it." 1993.

Fisherman's Talk*

The following is an afternoon encounter in two parts. This face-to-face conversation is from *Inport*, a publication from the Port of Seattle where people come to fish and enjoy casual small talk. Each student in class will be given a copy of this dialogue (without the translation) in order to follow the exchange between the fishermen. Two volunteers should read these parts. Joe talks first and Sam responds.

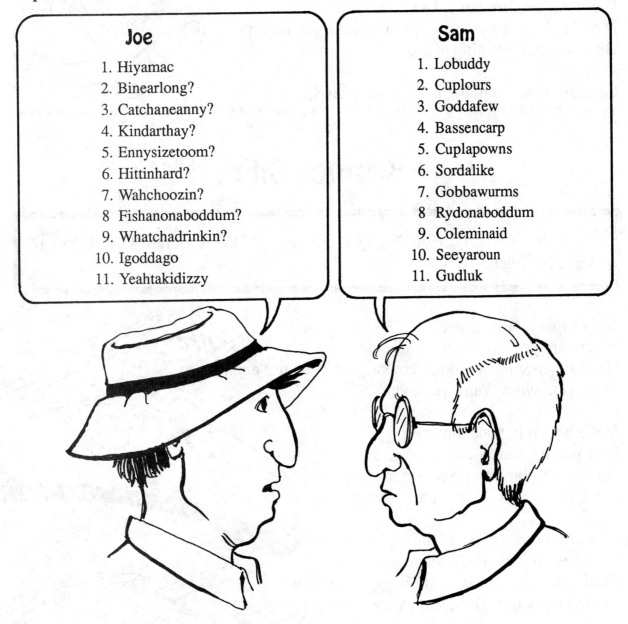

Joe

1. Hiyamac
2. Binearlong?
3. Catchaneanny?
4. Kindarthay?
5. Ennysizetoom?
6. Hittinhard?
7. Wahchoozin?
8. Fishanonaboddum?
9. Whatchadrinkin?
10. Igoddago
11. Yeahtakidizzy

Sam

1. Lobuddy
2. Cuplours
3. Goddafew
4. Bassencarp
5. Cuplapowns
6. Sordalike
7. Gobbawurms
8. Rydonaboddum
9. Coleminaid
10. Seeyaroun
11. Gudluk

Try this difficult trick of writing phrases with an inner ear attuned to the slurred sounds we actually use in conversation. Wujasay?

---

* Ibid.

Frére Jacques

The greatest thing about singing a round is that everyone can participate! The total effect is gratifying, and all kinds of voices will do just fine. Frére Jacques is most familiar, while the novel adaptation below works just as well. Try both of them and if you feel inspired, don't hesitate to compose your own original round.

Are you sleeping, are you sleeping,
Brother John, Brother John?
Morning bells are ringing, morning bells are ringing,
Ding, dong, ding; ding, dong ding.

German: Bim, bam, bom; bim, bam, bom.
****

Brother Billy

Dedicated to Billy, Hot Dog Man Emeritus, Athens Coney Island, Royal Oak, Michigan

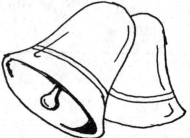

Billy Lipsey, Billy Lipsey
Where are you, where are you?
Cooking up some hot dogs, cooking up some hot dogs
Yum, yum, yum; Yum, yum, yum.

Make hot chili, make hot chili
Like you do, like you do
Serve it in a big bowl, serve it in a big bowl,
Yum, yum, yum; Yum, yum, yum.

Mustard onions, mustard onions
Gold french fries, gold french fries
Chili dogs are luscious, chili dogs are luscious
Yum, yum, yum; Yum, yum, yum.

GA1513

Garbled Story

We have all had the experience of listening to a joke or a story told by one person and later hearing the "same" story told much differently by another person. Perhaps the retelling varies because of style. Maybe our memory is not quite accurate or perhaps it is because we all process information in dissimilar ways.

We will try to reconstruct this experience with the entire class acting as the audience. If things work well, the variation in details in the story's retelling from one teller to the next can be funny, or confusing, or the entire story may be completely changed around.

Directions:

1. The teacher selects a very short story (see the following folktale) which has a few strong or dramatic details to be kept straight.
2. Three volunteer storytellers stand in front of the room as the teacher reads the story to the class.
3. After the reading, Teller number one tells the story as he or she remembers it.
4. Then, Teller two tells the story as he or she remembers it.
5. Finally, Teller three tells the story as he or she remembers it.

By this time, unless everyone is perfect, the story is considerably garbled and everyone has had a novel and telling experience.

> If you were a teller, what problems would you have had?

The teacher can customize this activity to fit class needs. Use fewer tellers, find a shorter anecdote, or do whatever makes it effective for your class.

The following is an example of the kind of short story, traditional or contemporary, which can be used effectively.

GA1513

Example:

Garbled Story
A Retold Russian Folktale

It was a savage winter in the Russian countryside. A pathetic little sparrow was lying at the side of the road desperately cold. There was no one around to help as it waited for the miserable end to its wretched suffering.

All at once a peasant appeared on his way to market. He saw the little bird and sincerely wanted to save its life. He looked everywhere but couldn't find a thing to wrap around the frail little creature to protect it from the brutal cold–there wasn't a rag or a shred of paper–then all at once he was inspired with an idea. He scooped up some straw and dirt, mixed them together with snow and packed the bird tightly in a mud blanket. Satisfied that he had saved the life of the tiny creature, he left the bird at the side of the road and walked off with a lighter heart!

Indeed, the bird was overwhelmed by the mud that held him in its life-giving warmth. He wanted to open his beak and sing to the sky for joy. But he was not quite strong enough to burst into song. Instead, the sounds that came out of his throat were not musical at all but were feeble and strange squawks.

Just then an old woman came by and heard the little bird's squawking noises, which she believed were a cry for help. Obviously he was in pain. "Oh my goodness," said the old woman, "Let me get you out of that prison of mud." Scraping and clawing diligently, she freed him of the mud. What a pleasure to have done a good deed, she thought. Satisfied, she placed him tenderly at the side of the road.

As you would expect, the little bird was, once again, completely exposed to the wind and the cold. Unhappily, within hours he froze to death.

There are three morals to this sad, muddy story:

Number 1: It is not necessarily your enemies who put you in it.
Number 2: It is not necessarily your friends who take you out.
Number 3: If you are in it up to your neck, for goodness sake, don't sing!

Gorilla Sting

This exercise requires some lead time. Give yourself a few days to look over the newspapers and magazines at school or at home. Find an appropriate article of strong personal interest to you. The item may come from any section of the publication, even an advertisement which is intriguing. After teacher approval, cut out the item and paste it at the top of a piece of paper, leaving room for your commentary below. What was it in the article that captured your attention? Is it controversial, humorous, informative, or astonishing? Volunteer to read your news item to the class. As with all good research, include the specifics of the source that was used. Include the name of the publication, the date, the section, the page, and a byline (journalist's name) if it was included.

Example:

Newsbrief Magazine

"Don't Monkey Around"

You may not know much about the exploits of the U.S. Fish and Wildlife Agency, but its agents are hard at work protecting the laws of the land from illegal monkey business. This adventure, reported by U.S. Attorney Dan Gelber, sounds as if it were taken right out of a movie scene from *Tarzan and the Apes*. The agents in Miami were involved in a sting operation with a certain Mexican Director of Zoos, Victor Bernal, who arranged to buy two primates which he planned to smuggle illegally across the border. One of the two gorillas was replaced by a very large U.S. agent all dressed up in a gorilla suit. When the meeting took place, the cage was opened and the "smaller" gorilla seemed so vicious and threatening that he frightened the zookeeper, Mr. Bernal. When the monkeyshines were over, the agent stepped out of his costume and arrested the zookeeper who was promptly taken into custody.*

---

* This story is a paraphrase of an item which was on all the news wires, the week of February 8, 1993, and was detailed in the feature, "That's Life," *Newsweek* magazine, page 59.

GA1513

Guess a Birthday

Tell a partner that you are about to use magic to guess his or her birthday! Ask the birthday person to do some easy magical (accurate) arithmetic according to your direction. When the arithmetic is complete, look at the results carefully and the day and date of the birthday answer will be revealed to you.

Directions to the Birthday Person:

A. At the top of your paper write the number of the month and day you were born.
B. Skip a line.
C. Now multiply the number of the month you were born by 5.
D. Add 6.
E. Multiply that number by 4.
F. Add 9.
G. Multiply by 5.
H. Add the day of your birth.
 I. Subtract 165.

Solution:

The last two digits on the right represent the day of birth, and the first digits to the left represent the month of birth.

Example:

A. My Birthday is October 23 or 10/23
B. Skip a line
C. 5 x 10 = 50
D. 6 + 50 = 56
E. 4 x 56 = 224
F. 9 + 224 = 233
G. 5 x 233 = 1165
H. 23 + 1165 = 1188
 I. 1188 - 165 = 1023 or 10/23 or October 23!

GA1513

Hair

I Worship at the Altar of Hair

High and curly
wavy, swirly
Long and short and fluffy poo

Kinky, springy
Straight and stringy
Thick and thin and bleached so true

Permanenté-eleganté
Dyed and fried
And conked all through

Braided, mohawked,
Scalped and frazzled
Tell the world that I love you.

Brains and soul may tell a story
But hair is still my crowning glory!
Comb it
Brush it
Clip it
Puff it
Mousse and tease it
Dunk and squeeze it

How about a nice shampoo?

Greta B. Lipson

Attention all hair lovers! Hair is associated with youth, strength, self-expression, and even romance. In history and literature, long hair has often had an androgynous quality (having the characteristics of both male and female).

Imagine you, or a group of students, write copy for a high-powered advertising agency. Launch a selling campaign for all kinds of hair products! Use names from the past and present to emphasize your message: Samson from the Bible, Rapunzel from fairy tales, Medusa from Greek mythology, Lady Godiva from eleventh-century England, and King Louis XIV from France.

* *Audacious Poetry* (GA1417), by Greta B. Lipson, © 1992, Good Apple, Carthage, Illinois.

GA1513

Hats Off!

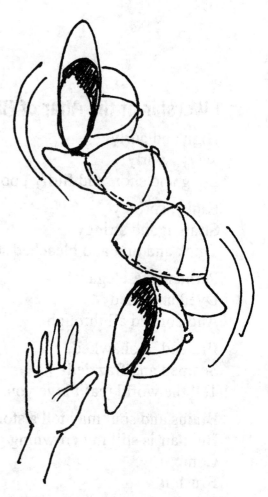

When we say to a friend or acquaintance "My hat's off to you," it is a sign of respect, admiration, or high regard for something well done. We don't literally doff our hats because, mainly, we hardly ever wear hats anymore–but the hat we tip is symbolic. It is an old-time figure of speech, but no matter how old, it still carries a great message which is wonderful to send or receive.

Because "Hats Off" is such an important tribute, it can be sent to classmates, teachers, principals, school volunteers, school staff, or members of the community who have earned respect. Decide who in your school community deserves the recognition of your class. Send out notices of a special day to honor a praiseworthy person, but don't reveal the entire plan because there will be a big fun surprise as part of the event!

The surprise is this: Prepare a banner for "Hats Off Day" in honor of that very special person of your choice. Have a ceremony with every class member (including the teacher) sporting a wildly artistic hat. Everyone in class will find, dig up, mooch, or borrow an old hat. It doesn't matter whether it is a man's or a woman's hat because the hats are to be trimmed so extravagantly–with such color and panache–that it won't matter what they looked like originally.

The ideas that spin off from this are incredible to contemplate. You could ask permission to hold a "Hats Off" assembly where speakers honor the recipient, who faces an audience of hats. Consider a parade on school grounds to celebrate the honorable recipient. Design an award for your honoree that will mark this special day. Have an award for the most outrageous chapeau!

Make "Hats Off Day" a tradition that starts with your class, now! Use your imagination! The sky is the limit. Alert the media! (Spread the good cheer and send pictures of some of the madcap hat creations to G. Lipson, P.O. Box 3452, Ann Arbor, MI 48106)

Hexaduad Poetry

This poetic form is made up of six couplets. A couplet is defined as two lines of verse which rhyme and express a complete thought. The hexaduad tells its complete story in twelve entertaining rhymed lines. Read this poem over, analyze it, and then try to compose your own hexaduad poem. Select a subject which has strong, humorous, or dramatic possibilities. Make sure the entire hexaduad makes sense. A funny topic may be easier for your first effort, but don't hesitate to try a serious topic!

My Cat Is Gone!

Have you seen my friendly cat?
He's handsome and he's fat.

His mood is always sunny
So I named him "Mr. Honey."

He hangs out in the alley
With his red-haired friend Ms. Sally.

One dark and rainy day
He slipped out the back way.

I miss him it is true
And his absence makes me blue.

I wait at home and sigh–
'Cause I think this means "good-bye."

GA1513

Hot Topics

We all have topics in mind which we would like to discuss (or hear others discuss) but how do we introduce these subjects without embarrassment? Here is a way to do it comfortably. Everyone in the class is invited to write down the title of a discussion topic to be handed in. The teacher will review these topics before the session begins. The name of the person who originated the subject will not be revealed. As the topic is announced, anyone can make a statement about it. The timer allows for three minutes per person. If someone does not take up the full amount of time, that person says "pass" and someone else may be heard. The total discussion time for a topic is five minutes.

Teenage Sex

DRUGS and ALCOHOL

Violence in the Movies

TV PROS and cons

ROCK MUSIC

Mandatory Service

Contributed by Ms. Cheryl Casola, Creighton Middle School, Phoenix, Arizona.

Hundred Dollar Gamble

Some smart guy known around town as Iggy the Gambler works number tricks all the time on everybody. He comes by one day and puts a proposition to me.

He says, "How would you like to earn a hundred dollars just by adding a column of figures?"

I, of course, replied, "Something here inside tells me there's a tough catch in there someplace. Since when are you giving away big bucks for so little effort?"

"Well," he says, "does that mean you'll take a challenge that takes so little effort? You see, this deal works both ways. Either you get the hundred dollars or if you can't make it happen, I get the money!"

I didn't know how to back out. He wasn't asking me to do anything illegal, and it sounded simple enough. Besides, a few of the guys were around and I didn't feel like being embarrassed again, so I said, "OK. Give me your riddle so I can earn this easy money. What do I have to do?"

"Well," Iggy says, smiling his big smile, "here are your directions":

- Add a column of double-digit numbers and one single-digit number to total the sum of 100.
- All the numbers from 1 to 9 must appear in your addends.
- You can use each number only once.
- Add the column of figures and make necessary changes. Don't rush.

You have probably guessed that I worked for a long time and every time Iggy looked at what I was doing he kept shaking his head "No!" Exhausted and feeling dumb, I dared him to show me the solution.

Maybe you can figure it out.

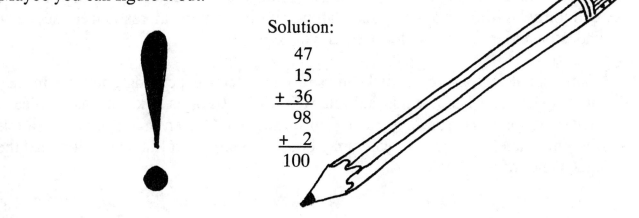

Solution:

$$
\begin{array}{r}
47 \\
15 \\
+\ 36 \\
\hline
98 \\
+\ 2 \\
\hline
100
\end{array}
$$

GA1513

I'm in a State

Can you describe or identify the following items as they relate to your own state? Every one of the fifty states in the union has the following items.

- A state seal
- A state bird
- A state flower
- A state tree
- A state capital
- A state song
- A state motto
- A state flag

After you research your own state, assume the role of a person who is responsible for making choices for a new state. Give the new state an imaginative, memorable name (the state of Confusion?). Work down the list of the items above and draw a seal, choose a bird, select a flower, or develop a hybrid . . . . Create each of these items and then top it off with a large illustration of a colorful state flag. Be artistic and daring!

If you were to write advertising copy to attract tourists to your new state, what would you say that would help bring in tourists and financial advantage to your economy? Think about the geography involved, natural resources, scenery, industry, and even state history. It's all yours to exploit.

Many people recognize the nicknames of other states depending upon where they have visited or where friends and relatives reside. Georgia is known as the Peach State, Florida is the Sunshine State, California is the Golden State, and Delaware is the First State. A review of geography books in your school library will reveal the nicknames of other states.

Interpret This Drawing

Look carefully at the busy illustration on the right. What are some of the details which you consider important? Who are the characters? How many are there and how do you perceive them? What activities are taking place? What is the interior or background for this gathering? Do you feel a sense of the mood in this place? Are you aware of danger, frivolity, humor, or sadness? Is the scene modern or historical? What title seems appropriate?

Having examined the picture, each of you may respond to these questions orally. Explain or write your impressions of the picture. If you are captivated by one section of the picture, you may focus on that alone. How many different interpretations are there in the class? Why doesn't everyone see the very same thing in the picture? What does this exercise tell us?

---

* *A Dictionary of Reading and Related Terms*, T.L. Harris & R.E. Hodges, Coeditors, International Reading Association, page 232, © 1981. Newark, Delaware. Used with permission.

Ironical Mask

Look up the definition of the term *irony*. It is defined as something you say when you actually mean the opposite. So the literal meaning is not your intended meaning. But sometimes a definition just makes things foggier. Here is an example of irony: If you are dog-tired and you say, "Boy, am I feeling peppy!"–you are using the technique of irony. Or if at midterm you say, "I really look forward to exams!" people understand that exam time is dreaded by everyone and your statement is ironic.

Examples:

- If the captain of the football team begs me to go on a date, I guess I'll have to force myself.
- I love making a fool of myself in front of the whole class.
- My mother says I don't have to clean my room this weekend. Boy, am I disappointed.
- It's no trouble at all to go miles out of my way to do you a favor instead of going to the beach with my friends on a gorgeous day.

Now it's your turn to list some ironical statements that you use or hear often. But this time, include in parentheses the true literal meaning behind the statement. What is the difference between spoken and written irony? (Answer: Spoken irony often presents more clues from the tone of voice and body language.)

GA1513

Isaac Asimov's Choice

> The following synopsis and activities are based upon Isaac Asimov's short story entitled "Evidence," from *I, Robot*.*

Cast of Characters

Stephen Byerly: A young, popular district attorney
Mr. Quinn: A concerned citizen
Dr. Lanning: Former director of U.S. Robot & Mechanical Men Corp.
Dr. Susan Calvin: A respected robopsychologist

Synopsis:

Imagine a time far in the future in a typical American city where an election for mayor is about to take place. The principal candidate for the office, Stephen Byerly, is a brilliant, young district attorney. His qualifications are sterling, and he is widely admired as a very honorable and decent human being. He seems almost too good to be true!

Byerly's background is well known to everyone. He was born and raised in a small town, married young, and lived modestly with his wife and baby. Tragedy struck the little family early when an automobile accident took the lives of the mother and child. Stephen, whose injuries were severe, had a slow return to health. Once recovered, he went to law school, moved to the big city, and pursued a successful career as an attorney. There were no surprises in his straightforward career.

In the course of Steve Byerly's campaign activity, a certain Mr. Quinn (who is not running for office) is asking some very probing questions about the young candidate and is circulating some bizarre rumors as well. He justifies his tactics by saying that it is useful to investigate the lives of "reform politicians." He publicly asks the question: Why has Steve Byerly, the energetic district attorney, never, ever been seen eating, drinking, or sleeping?

---

* Original copyright, 1950, Gnome Press. Doubleday, © 1963, Garden City, N.Y.

Quinn, as a concerned citizen, meets with the distinguished Dr. Lanning, the former Director of Research of the U.S. Robot & Mechanical Men Corporation. The robotics industry has flourished in the city for many years under a closely regulated government program which severely regulates the use of robots. The company steadfastly remains free of political involvements.

Dr. Lanning is outraged with Quinn's implication that Steve Byerly is too good to be human and is perhaps a robot manufactured illegally in his factory! The scientist makes it clear that the corporation has never developed, nor do they have the capacity to produce, a humanoid-looking robot with a superior positronic brain!

The company would be driven out of business by the authorities if it dared tamper with such experimentation! According to the law, the company is held responsible for the actions of its more advanced technology, which is leased but never sold! The old roboticist perceives Mr. Quinn's accusation as a veiled threat.

Quinn suggests to Dr. Lanning that it is in the best interests of the company to prove that Steve Byerly is human and is not a highly sophisticated, illegal mechanical man produced by the company. Quinn further suggests that if Lanning refuses to cooperate in this effort, the U.S. Robot Corporation will be accused of knowingly committing a crime against the citizens of the metropolis for profit.

Quinn insists that if Dr. Lanning will simply make Steve Byerly eat something, to demonstrate that he is human, the corporation will be off the hook and Quinn will be satisfied that Steve is not a robot.

With his back against the wall, Dr. Lanning calls in Dr. Susan Calvin, a respected robopsychologist in the robotics industry asking for her advice and participation. She is known to hold a most favorable view of robots because their behavior is programmed to hold to a standard of ethics that does not yield to the weakness of human corruption.

Steve Byerly resists Mr. Quinn's insistence that he eat publicly! The young candidate charges that these demands are political shenanigans in violation of his civil rights! He states his objections convincingly with Quinn, Lanning, and Susan Calvin present.

Exasperated, Steve finally yields and eats an apple from Dr. Susan Calvin's purse to put an end to the nonsense! She reminds those present that if any technology was capable of producing a robot so refined that it could fool other humans, then the processes of eating, drinking, and sleeping would certainly be included as safety features to protect the security of the humanoid robot to defy detection!

GA1513

Consider This:

• What questions and concerns would you want to discuss before deciding to vote for Stephen Byerly to be the mayor of your city?

• If it were proven that a robot, because of its incorruptibility and superior ability to process data, was more fit to govern than a human, what doubts might you still have?

• Choose up campaign sides for and against Steve Byerly's candidacy for mayor. Give each side a chance to express their views and convince the audience of voters. Conduct a closed election following the speeches.

• How could the "Robot Code of Ethics" be regarded as a religion? What do you think of the code?

GA1513

The Three Laws in the Robot Code of Ethics

First Law: Human life must be protected from harm.

Second Law: An order given by a human must be obeyed unless it threatens human life.

Third Law: A robot must protect its own existence, but only if it does not come in conflict with the first or second law.

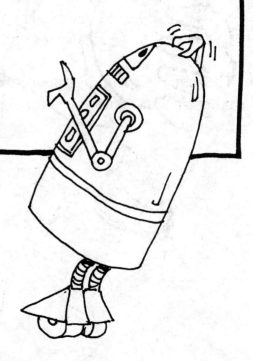

GA1513

Just Say "Oh"

Every form of communication has its own special characteristics. When we are listening to spoken language we can tell the meaning that is intended by the delivery, the pitch, the mood–the complete sound made by the speaker. If one were to capture the same scene in writing, it would require much more explanation, such as "Betsy said, 'Oh' with great sympathy," or "Harry's response was a simple 'Oh' in his usual haughty way," or "The children said 'Oh' and sounded suspicious of the situation." A demonstration of this can be set up by asking a student to read aloud a series of sentences (all with different meanings) to which the single response is the word *oh*.

One person at a time may respond to the following statements with the word *oh*. If the class thinks the response is incorrect, have another person respond to the same question until there is agreement about the sound of the mood.

- Look at those cute puppies!
- The police are here!
- You're hired.
- I just saw a big, brown rat.
- Would you like a piece of chocolate cream pie?
- There's a deep, dark pit just inches away from your feet.
- Are you really hungry?
- They just kissed and made up.
- You will be grounded for one month.

The same listening exercise can be created using other words or sentences. What other choices can your class develop to which the tone of the response gives the meaning?

GA1513

Lai Verse

There is nothing freewheeling about this verse form! It has a highly "restricted" pattern which is guaranteed to frustrate anyone who tries to compose it. Trying to write a Lai verse is like trying to create a new dance step while being restrained in the confines of a narrow box. Writing such a poem is an exasperating puzzle, but there are some of us who love puzzles.

The Lai poem has nine lines and only two rhyme schemes. It is also based upon a five- and two-syllable rhythm. It looks like this:

Are You Here?

5 syllables	Is it you I hear	a
5	Down the lonely years	a
2	I dream.	b
5 syllables	Your voice is so clear	a
5	So strong and so near	a
2	A beam!	b
5 syllables	I touch you, my dear	a
5	My fear disappears	a
2	Serene.	b

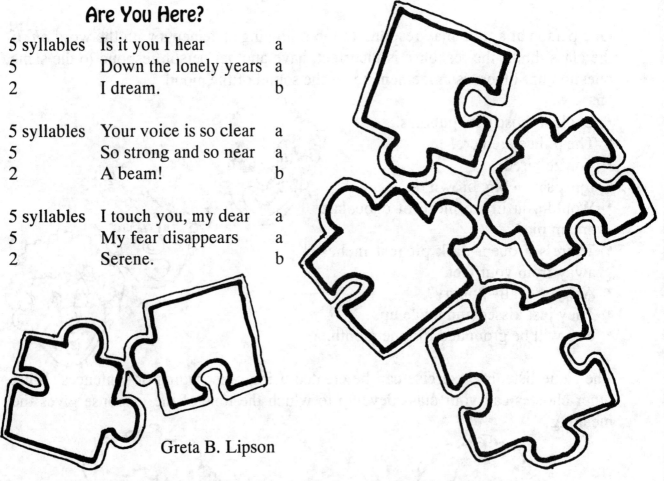

Greta B. Lipson

If you are up to the challenge, here are some clues that might help.

1. First, your poem must make sense, and that is difficult.
2. Make several lists of words which have the most rhyming possibilities.
   - *tranquil, bill, sill, mill, hill, drill, grill, still, fill, spill, nil*
   - *sky, try, buy, fly, high, guy, dry, spy, decry, cry*
3. Choose the list that has possibilities for a theme, a story, or a statement.
4. Plan line #1 and line #3 because these two lines are your rhyme scheme.

54

5. One last suggestion which may rescue you from total frustration: If you are having trouble with the two-syllable words, you may use the same line in each verse as if it were a refrain (see "I dream," below).

Are You Here?

Is it you I hear
Down the lonely years
I dream.

Your voice is so clear
So strong and so near
I dream.

I touch you my dear
My fear disappears
I dream.

I had never encountered Lai verse until I read Ruth K. Carlson's *Sparkling Words*. She had found it in a book, *The Hollow Reed*, by Mary J.J. Wrinn, copyrighted in 1935 by Harper Brothers. Because the form is so rare, it is appropriate to include the source.

GA1513

Magic Pen

There had never been a better birthday party for my twin sister and me. The two of us, Mandy and Mark, are fraternal twins which means we are not identical–we don't look alike and she is a girl. The family has always been great about birthday presents. Everyone seems to understand that we both share similar interests and skills, so the gifts are things we can both use.

After the party Mandy's share of the cleanup job is done, and she is already outside playing with the new baseball mitt. I'm always slower and am finally throwing away all the birthday gift wrappings. All at once I spot a small, elegantly wrapped package still on the table. How could we have missed it, especially since the color of the paper is iridescent? In fact the paper looks like a hologram. It is doing truly strange things under the light. It flashes and changes, suggesting images and forms that slip away from my mind's eye.

I decide not to ask anyone about this present and proceed to unwrap it slowly, as all the while the colors keep shimmering and reflecting light. Inside the box I find a pen that looks like an old-fashioned ink pen or a stylus. I'm not sure. I keep turning it over and over and decide to try it out. Sometimes, when I'm alone I talk out loud, and this time I hear myself say, "This is an opportunity to write a thank-you note to our family friend, Jim, who baked our sensational birthday cake!"

I grab a piece of loose-leaf paper and, at the very same second, I actually watch that pen perk up and begin to write IN MY HANDWRITING! The finished note is a rare beauty! The spelling is correct, the words wonderfully chosen, and–what's even greater–it makes me sound like a genius! A few more notes and I realize the pen translates my wishes into its commands. Each written note is beautifully crafted. Imagine the possibilities for homework assignments, taking tests, writing for profit, personal and business letters.

56

The Big Ethical Questions for the Reader to Answer:

- How could this pen mean fame and fortune for Mark?
- How could this pen bring trouble and misadventures?
- How could this pen complicate Mark's life?
- How could this pen be used in ways that would benefit others?
- Do you think the pen has its own intelligence? Why?

Major Event

Almost each and every one of us has experienced a major event in our lives which we know we will never forget! Perhaps it occurred years ago or only yesterday. It may have lasted five minutes, an hour, or a full day. It may have been an incredibly happy event, a moment full of pride, or a time that was desperately sad or frightening.

Think back and reflect on your major event. Give yourself a chance to remember. Write some notes that will help you recollect every detail. Don't rush. Make the experience vivid so that the reader, too, feels the scope and intensity of your emotions. (The teacher may want to model this assignment with a finished essay of his or her own major event.)

GA1513

Me, Myself, and I

Use every letter of the alphabet to develop a series of complete sentences which describe your personality as fully as possible. Underline every consecutive letter of the alphabet which helps define your character and interests. The fun part is that the alphabetical word can be anywhere in the sentence. Don't be modest. You can flesh out the statement in a way that truly captures your personality, and do remember to include your first and last name somewhere, as follows:

Me, Myself, and I

A   The kids call me <u>Amanda</u> the athlete.
B   I have been called a <u>baseball</u> freak at school.
C   My voice can be heard loud and clear in the <u>choir</u>.
D   My oldest and dearest friend is my <u>dog</u> Huxtable.
E   I want to be an electrical <u>engineer</u> when I grow up.
F   The all-time greatest day of the week for me is <u>Friday</u>!
G   My last name is <u>Garcia</u>, like my smart, strong grandmother.

GA1513

Midway–Choral Speaking

Parts:

1. Kids: "This is neat. It can't be beat."
2. Old Folks: "Isn't that nice."
3. Tunnel of Love: "Huggy, kissy"
4. Roller Coaster: "Clickety clack, clickety clack–whoosh"
5. Barker: "Step right up."
6. Snake Charmer:

Directions:

Select a group for every part listed. Pass out the script of "Midway" to everyone. Assign one sound effect to each group. Allow for rehearsal time. The teacher-narrator begins as everyone reads along silently. When each group hears its name, they stand and make their sound immediately. The narrator will ask to hear the sounds of each group once before starting. Suggestions for more dramatic effects after the first rehearsal will be welcome. Make any changes in characters, things, and events which please the class after the performances.

Midway

Sunday at the state fair was the most exciting time of the year for the KIDS and the OLD FOLKS. The colorful Ferris wheel turned on its way up to the sky and down again, romance beckoned from the TUNNEL OF LOVE, and the ROLLER COASTER stopped to load up with more people. Many drifted to the midway to listen to the BARKER. He invited one and all to pay admission to see the tattooed man, the bearded lady, and the calf with two heads. By far the most alluring act of all was the SNAKE CHARMER with her gleaming reptile, half-coiled in a basket with its gorgeous head swaying enough to put the crowd in a trance. And all of this for only fifty cents!

The BARKER commanded the attention of the KIDS and the OLD FOLKS as the group of performers moved onstage doing just enough to tease the customers into the tent. The SNAKE CHARMER did not seem to notice that her treacherous-looking snake began to slither up one leg. Slowly, silently, he was circling and binding both her legs together. Up and up the sinuous serpent moved silently from her hips to her waist to her shoulders. The BARKER continued his spiel while the KIDS and OLD FOLKS watched with popping eyes! This was indeed a hideous turn of events!

GA1513

People coming out of the TUNNEL OF LOVE saw immediately what was happening and rushed toward the stage. The ROLLER COASTER slowed to a halt as the crowds began to shout. This snake was serious and meant to do deadly physical harm! All at once, a young, strong girl ripped through the crowd. She ran toward the SNAKE CHARMER who was turning blue in the face from the stranglehold of the snake at her throat. The OLD FOLKS cleared a path for the schoolgirl. Very gently, standing on tiptoes, she whispered sweet, crooning words to the snake. He loosened his powerful coils as if he were hypnotized and dropped back into his basket like a slack rope.

The passengers on the ROLLER COASTER roared their gratitude to the little girl! The TUNNEL OF LOVE customers cheered her as a hero, and the relieved BARKER offered free candy floss and taffy apples for everybody. And so he enjoyed the approval of the KIDS, the SNAKE CHARMER, the passengers from the TUNNEL OF LOVE, the customers on the ROLLER COASTER, and the OLD FOLKS!

ALL VOICES:

All's well that ends well.

GA1513

More Derived Sentences

For this writing exercise select a strong, colorful noun (a person, place, or thing) which has creative possibilities! Try out the strength of this noun as you proceed with the following steps:

- Use this noun in six sentences.
- Each sentence must have six words.
- The noun must be used in first, second, third, fourth, fifth, and sixth places consecutively.
- Use different words in each sentence.
- The sentences must make sense.
- If you don't like the effect of the noun, try another one.

Dracula

1. DRACULA is a spooky, villainous bloodsucker.
2. Wicked DRACULA is a loathsome character.
3. Evil Count DRACULA cannot be trusted.
4. Have you seen DRACULA around town?
5. I am afraid vile DRACULA vanished.
6. A holy object will scare DRACULA.

GA1513

Mrs. Padgett's Roomer

It had been a lucky day when Henry found a reasonable room to rent in Mrs. Padgett's rooming house. He could hardly pay the kind of rent others were paying in the neighborhood; yet he wanted desperately to make it on his own. The weekly paycheck at Hagler's Hardware wasn't much to live on but it was a start.

Mrs. Padgett, the landlady, ran an unforgiving household and everyone cooperated out of gratitude for the modest rental. She had enough rules to frighten an army sergeant. No food was to be hidden in the rooms. No friends after 8 p.m. No alcoholic beverages, and no disturbing laughter. Henry tried his best to stay on her good side. Actually his life depended on it.

He was especially nervous about the bathroom rules. One always had to leave the bathroom spotlessly clean! Mrs. Padgett had publicly humiliated one of her roomers more than once, after her "cleanliness inspection." When it was Henry's turn for a bath on Saturday night he was painfully careful. He tiptoed on the floor because her rooms were right below.

Once in the tub he relaxed and felt the warm water bubble out of the faucet in a welcome stream. The heat enveloped his body as it slowly renewed his tense muscles and weary spirit. If he ever became rich, Henry vowed, he would take a steaming, soapy bath every single night of the week and soak until his skin wrinkled.

During his reverie, the bath had reached a pleasant level and he bent forward to turn off the water. The faucet did not respond. He tried with more muscle, grasping the handle tightly and turning it clockwise. Still the water did not stop. The sweat began to pop out on his upper lip as he used both hands now. His knuckles turned white with the effort. Still nothing loosened. The water kept up its steady, relentless gushing. No amount of frenzied twisting or turning produced results! The wanton energy of the flow was causing a pounding in his head!

The water rose higher and soon would spill full force over the tub. It would quickly cover the floor and cascade down in a great sopping, destructive flood into Mrs. Padgett's sitting room below! Henry's panic mounted. She would throw him out! He would have to pay a fortune for the damage he had caused! He could never recover from such a financial disaster! Powerless, he slumped–disconsolate in the raging water. Henry considered drowning himself as an escape from his miserable fate. The sloshing water was brimming unabated–almost even now with the edge of the porcelain tub!

The Big Questions:

• What would you have done? (How about pulling the plug on the bathtub drain?)
• Identify the words, sentences, or phrases which create a mounting sense of disaster in this selection.

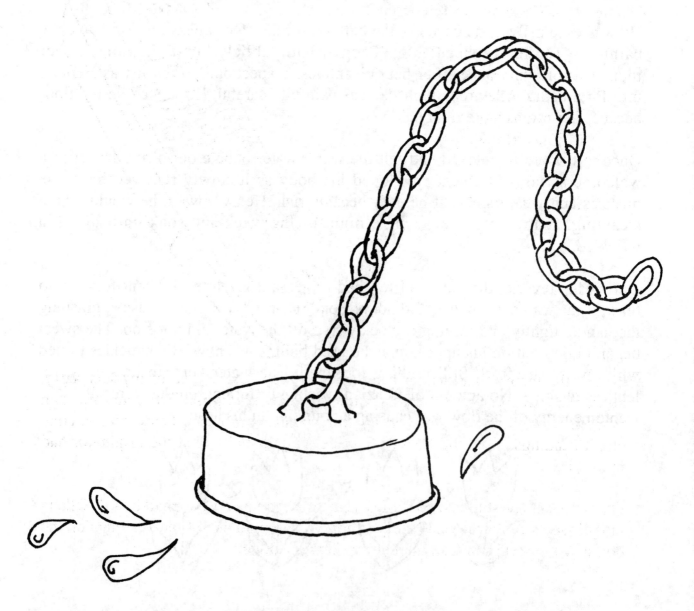

GA1513

Mystery Chapters

You have written a complicated mystery story and you think it is sensational. It is rather long but it moves along at a hair-raising pace. You submit the finished manuscript to your editor at the Eerie Publishing Company and she really likes it! She suggests that it would be helpful to readers if you would divide the story into ten chapters. The title of each chapter would help give clues to the strange sequence and twists and turns of the story plot. You give a title to each chapter and quickly realize that the chapter headings could become unified into many different mystery stories!

Give a title to five or ten chapters keeping a story in mind.

Example:

Chapter 1. A Voice on the Telephone
2. Interviews at the Circus
3. The Body in the Cannon!
4. A Suspect at Last
5. Blind Alley
6. Back to Square One
7. The Grim Reaper
8. New Evidence
9. A Ghastly Mask
10. The Truth Will Come Out

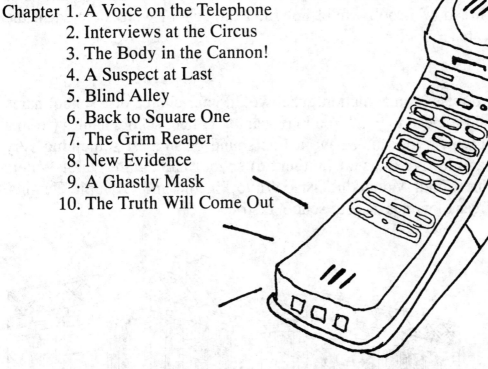

• To test the theory that chapter headings can become any kind of mystery story, students will exchange their written chapter headings. Then, anyone can volunteer to tell a short story orally, in a spontaneous effort, based on someone else's headings. How did the creative ideas compare to what the originator had in mind?

• Or, two or three students could list chapter headings on the chalkboard. Others in their seats can write out a story synopsis, based on one of the headings on the board. Volunteers can read their story sketches aloud.

GA1513

Name a Great School

There was a time when schools were named for Presidents, poets, authors, or women and men of achievement nationally or on a local or state level. Sometimes if a beloved principal retired, the school then took on that person's name as a way of honoring a dedicated educator.

But these days, if you do any traveling, it becomes apparent that schools are named in many different ways which are refreshing changes from the usual custom of using surnames. It could be a challenge to give a school a name that really reflects a community, the neighborhood spirit, or something unique about the geographic location. Of course, it is also true that neighborhoods change, and later a name such as Meadow Brook would not fit if the school were situated in the heart of an urban area.

Since this is an exercise in imagination, what would your choice of a school name be, and what would it mean to you? You may want to collect school names (from a school directory) which you think have a fine sound or suggest something very pleasant. For example five unusual (authentic) school names are Quiet Waters Elementary, Divine Child, Mountain Vista, White Pigeon, and Olympia Heights. Research the sources of names in your school district.

66

Name That Movie*

In the history of the movies, the style in titles keeps changing in very interesting ways. Perhaps the most punchy titles are the hard-hitting, rhythmic ones, which are described as trochaic. A trochee (TROH-kee) has two syllables. The first syllable is stressed and the second one is unstressed (as in "young-er"). To develop a list of sure-fire movie titles, start with a trochaic adjective and end with a trochaic noun.

- Rotten   Apple
- Ghostly   Justice
- Monster   Rally
- Gonzo   Clamor
- Evil   Hipster
- Deadly   Recall
- Magic   Weapon

The fun part is that these titles can be used interchangeably as follows: Simply connect any word from the first list to any word in the second list. Rotten Apple becomes Rotten Hipster, Gonzo Clamor becomes Gonzo Weapon. You may also choose to forget about trochaic rhythm and form two lists side by side that offer other interesting possibilities.

- Doofus   Demons
- Ghostly   Whirligig
- Hamlet's   Booties
- Palooza's   Escapades

Who are the actors starring in your movie? Describe the movie in one sentence.

---

* From a suggestion in *The New York Times*, Sunday, June 21, 1992, Page H 13, by Jeffrey McQuain, William Safire's research associate, who writes the syndicated column "Our Language."

GA1513

Necklace

One day in English class, Ms. Barclay read her students a short story entitled "The Necklace" by the French author Guy de Maupassant (1850-1893). A synopsis appears on the following page.

This story, considered to be the author's most famous, has a strange twist to the ending–and on that particular day Ms. Barclay's students were very annoyed with it!

"Why do authors have to write a story with an ending that just hangs there and isn't really an ending?" they demanded to know. As a matter of fact, they were so indignant they insisted that they be allowed to do some rewriting and give the story the ending it deserved.

"All right," Ms. Barclay said. "It's your choice to improve on de Maupassant, so I'll help you along with one key sentence that will allow for your preferred ending!"

"After Madame Forestier revealed the truth about the necklace to the dispirited Mathilde–the poor woman left the boulevard and . . . ."

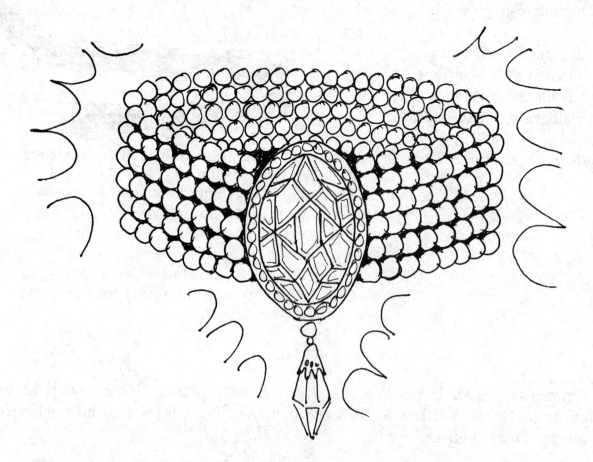

Synopsis: The Necklace

Madame Mathilde Loisel is married to a lowly clerk employed in the Ministry of Education. They are poor and barely manage to get by–a fact of life which makes the beautiful, young Mathilde utterly miserable. One day her husband brings home an invitation to a reception at the Ministerial mansion which he hopes will please her. She fumes and complains bitterly about having nothing to wear. He indulges her and gives her money he has saved–which is more than they can afford, to buy a party dress.

Mathilde still is not satisfied and complains that she needs jewelry. Her husband urges her to go to her generous friend Madam Forestier to borrow a jewel to enhance her dress. Her friend offers a splendid assortment from which Mathilde carefully selects a superb diamond necklace. The beautiful young woman is breathtaking in her new dress and necklace. At the party she attracts the admiration and attention of everyone present and is blissfully happy.

Back home, at four in the morning, she takes off her cloak and discovers that the necklace is no longer around her neck. Mathilde and her husband are both shocked and in despair when they are forced to have another diamond necklace made up which they can return to Madam Forestier. In order to scrape the money together, their lives become a nightmare of hardship, loans, misery, and poverty.

For ten years they live in an attic, and between them they are enslaved by debt. Their misfortune and desperately hard work takes its toll. Mathilde looks like an old, coarsened woman.

One day while walking on the main avenue of Paris she sees Madame Jeanne Forestier, who still looks young and lovely. Jeanne does not recognize this old woman from the past, but Mathilde introduces herself again. The friend inquires about Mathilde's poor condition, and the old woman tells the story of having had to work day and night to be able to replace the diamond necklace–whereupon Madame Forestier says, "Oh my poor Mathilde. But my necklace wasn't real–it was only an imitation!"

GA1513

Necromancer

However hard I look, I still cannot find this story in any collection. All this time I thought my sister had told it to me years ago. When I asked her recently, she said that it was I who had told it to her. It is a puzzlement. Neither of us knows its source though we guess that it comes from folklore. The important thing about this story is that it made a strong impression on us which neither of us has forgotten. And that is why I want to tell it to you.

There was a young man named Brendan Connaught who had fallen madly in love with Caitlin, a lovely young woman who lived down the lane. No matter how he tried to attract her attention, she barely knew he was alive. He felt such frustration that he was desperate for advice that would help in his campaign to make her aware of him. But nothing he did mattered. When he said hello she barely acknowledged him. She would look in another direction, or was absorbed in conversation. Caitlin wasn't mean; she was just busy. If they encountered each other face-to-face he would flash his most winning smile. If she smiled back he was sure it was not intended for him.

But one day his luck changed, when Travis, an old family friend, came visiting. "I read desperation in that long, sour face of yours. What could possibly be so bad, my boy?"

Brendan's frustration over Caitlin came spilling out. "I had hoped for a casual meeting and a warm awakening on her part. But it was never intended to be." He punctuated his remarks with hopeless sighs.

Travis was greatly distracted to see his young friend Brendan suffering so. "If you care deeply about this situation, why don't you consider a visit to Fenian, the chemist?" He smiled and winked, "I cannot speak from personal experience, but I have heard dark rumors that he practices a quiet magic with potions and such. I make no promises for Fenian, but perhaps it's worth a try." Travis left hoping that his little joke had lifted Brendan's spirits for the moment.

As you may have guessed, Brendan Connaught wasted no time on his way to Fenian's mysterious store. He trudged down the back roads, under the tracery of the trees' leafy shadows where the chemist's establishment was hidden from the brightness of sun and sky.

Brendan entered and was struck by an oppressive musty odor. Dust was everywhere, sifting down on the bottles of every hue that lined the walls. Every shape, every size. They stood like tired soldiers in tattered uniforms of cobwebs. They looked a hundred years old.

Brendan rang a small bell to summon the chemist. Did anyone from town actually come here? As he waited he strained to read the labels on the bottles but could not decipher them. Perhaps they were written in Latin. Fenian entered from the rear of the store. He was a spare, slight man with sympathetic eyes that invited a confidence. When he asked Brendan the nature of his business, he listened with the intensity of a kindly mentor.

The chemist asked many questions about Caitlin which the young man answered without embarrassment. Brendan wanted her to be his very own, to the exclusion of everyone and everything. He would make any sacrifice if she became his devoted, dedicated and loving wife, never to leave his side. He would be the sun in her universe. "I yearn for her affection."

"And you shall have it," replied Fenian, now that he had learned all that he needed to know to give Brendan what he wanted. The chemist turned his back and faced the shelves for a moment of contemplation. He moved swiftly from bottle to bottle, mixing here, stirring there, measuring with the precision of a man who knew exactly what had to be done. He worked in silence.

When the chemist was finished, he turned and wrapped the bottle in a piece of brown hand-torn paper. "The elixir will work. Read the directions and your wishes will come true."

Brendan beamed with gratitude. He put his hand in his pocket, "What is the cost, please, Mr. Fenian?"

"No need to pay, " the chemist said impassively.

"But I don't understand."

"You will only have to pay, young man, when you return. For now, sir, I bid you good day."

GA1513

The Big Questions:

1. Why would Brendan come back?
2. Why will he pay only when he returns?
3. How does Fenian, the chemist, earn his money?
4. What is this all about, anyway?

Possible Answers:

1. Brendan will be smothered by his loving wife, who never leaves his side. His life, devoid of friends, family, and outside interests, will be beyond his endurance.
2. Brendan will return for a potion to be released from the prison of his wife's overwhelming devotion, hoping to be granted some room to breathe! And for that favor he will have to pay a great deal of money.
3. Fenian earns money from people who desperately want their foolish wishes undone.
4. This is about having all one's wishes come true.

Many poets and authors have spoken to such a fantasy as in "The Monkey's Paw" by W.W. Jacobs. Do you agree or disagree with the following authors about fulfilled wishes?

- James Russell Lowell, a nineteenth-century poet, wrote, "Granting our wish is one of Fate's saddest jokes."
- Aesop said, "We would often be sorry if our wishes were gratified."
- Oscar Wilde, the Victorian playwright, said, "When the gods wish to punish us, they answer our prayers."
- Milton Covensky, Professor Emeritus of History, Wayne State University, said, "There are two tragedies in life. The first is not getting what you want. The second is getting it."

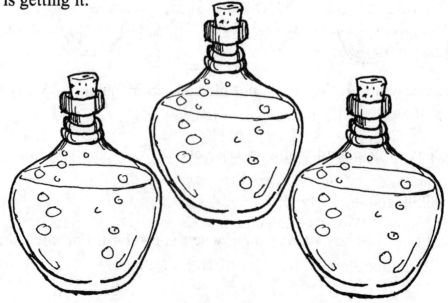

72

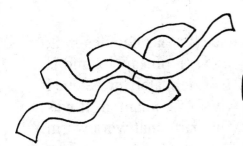

Noodle Mystery

It was a clever idea to have a cooking contest in Cooksville on a crisp Sunday afternoon in the winter. The price of admission was so cheap that entire families could attend. The judges were selected from the local newspaper, and since there were no name tags to identify the cooks, the judging would be fair and unbiased. Best of all there was to be an impressive cash prize!

A stream of cooks came into the community center in the morning while volunteers placed the delicious-looking dishes in the appropriate categories. It was a wonderful job for people who loved food. Now put the mouth-watering appetizers here, over there for the hearty soups and entrees, and toward the end of the table for glorious desserts. Each dish had an imaginative name, as one would expect, and was assigned a number and a proper place in its category.

People milled around, festive and eager for the event to commence when, in a serious and proper mood, the judges entered. The audience fell silent. It was hard to say what everyone would have given for the daunting job of tasting the foodstuffs on those tables! As in a tennis match, all eyes in the audience moved with the body language of the judges. Poised fork–to dish–to mouth–to taste centers in the brain–to revealing facial expressions. All of this was repeated over and over.

The room grew hotter and produced a mix of maddening food aromas. Time passed. The audience grew restless and there was a commotion. "What's happening?" everyone wanted to know from the buzz of the judges, now clutched in a private little conference.

Finally an announcement came, "The winner has been unanimously selected, but there is a serious hitch!" The crowd was disconcerted.

All the judges were bent over as they tried desperately to decipher the identifying sign leaning against the 9" x 13" baking dish. They squinted their eyes and scratched their heads. Clearly they could not read it. Did it say "Boogle" or "Google" or "Kugel"? Was it a main course, an appetizer, or a dessert?

"Describe it," someone shouted irritably from the audience.

GA1513

"Well," said the portly judge with the most eating experience, "it has noodles in it, and a sauce that would suggest cottage cheese. It's crunchy with pineapple, and is creamy in a way that coddles the palate like sour cream. It is delicately sweetened with golden raisins and it gives off the merest aromatic whiff of cinnamon. It was baked and can be cut into squares like a smooth dream. The parts that were warm were delicious and the parts that were cool were divine!"

The agitated crowd pressed forward for a decision, while the losing cooks could be recognized by their grim expressions of failure. The sponsors tried to pacify the crowd, "We promise you this: we will find the gifted cook who prepared this dish and award that person the generous cash prize as promised. But to demonstrate our appreciation and show our good faith we will get to the bottom of this noodle mystery. When it is solved we will publish the recipe in the newspaper for everyone to see. We pledge our determination to solve the mystery of this delicious Boogle, Google or Kugel, or whatever it is called!"

Dear Readers,

As part of our promise at the Cooksville cook-off we are asking you to try to help us identify this noodle dish! Please give it an appropriate name. As part of a class project (and because everybody loves a good recipe) bring your favorite recipes from home to organize into your own class collection. Name it "Food to Swoon Over."

---

* If you would like this prized noodle recipe to give to the cook in your life, write to G. Lipson, Box 3452, Ann Arbor, MI 48106.

74

GA1513

One More Chance

Context is the key to figuring out the strange words in the following letter. This activity may be done in a number of ways. It can be a whole class activity with oral participation with someone at the chalkboard recording the correct words. Or, it can be an individual writing activity for each student. In order to bring some meaning to the following paragraph, one letter must be added to the beginning or the ending of each senseless word that is encountered in the paragraph.

Ear teache,

I'm writing this etter to ask fo nother hance! I know hat I di was umb, but I couldn't elp yself. Sure, yo didn' ike the ay I cted but I ill do etter ext ime! I ust wanted to look ike a bi perso and it ot me int rouble! But I hav earned y esson. If ou orgive me his tim and don ive me fter chool detentio, I will neve ac like a bi ool gain! I romise!

You goo frien
ammy

The Straight Story:

Dear Teacher,

I'm writing this letter to ask for another chance! I know what I did was dumb, but I couldn't help myself. Sure, you didn't like the way I acted but I will do better next time! I just wanted to look like a big person and it got me into trouble! But I have learned my lesson. If you forgive me this time and don't give me after school detention, I will never act like a big fool again! I promise!

Your good friend,
Sammy or Tammy or ?

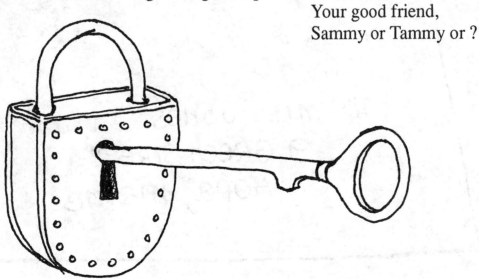

One Syllable

This is a game I would like you to play if you can. You can play if you see the point to all of this. Write a note to me but keep it short and sweet. Can you tell what I have done? You must do the same. You will have to use short words. You may not use long words at all. This task seems hard, but we do it to trick fools and give folks a hard time.

Hold to the rule of this task and you will win a smile. What is the point, you may ask. It is just a test of your skill and good brain. Did I hear you say it is a dumb game? I will not say you are wrong, but you must have a sense of fun. This plan can be hard if you make it that way. When you write your note back to me, it must make sense! But please do write as soon as you can. I wish you much luck and no sweat!

The Big Questions:
- Why is the writing so strange? (Answer: Every word has only one syllable.)
- What is the writer talking about? (Answer: The writer is challenging the reader to try to write a return letter with the same one-syllable rule.)
- Why isn't the writer more direct and understandable? (Answer: Her vocabulary is limited to one-syllable words.)
- Can you write a paragraph that makes sense with the limitation of using words of only one syllable? Try it, smart guy!

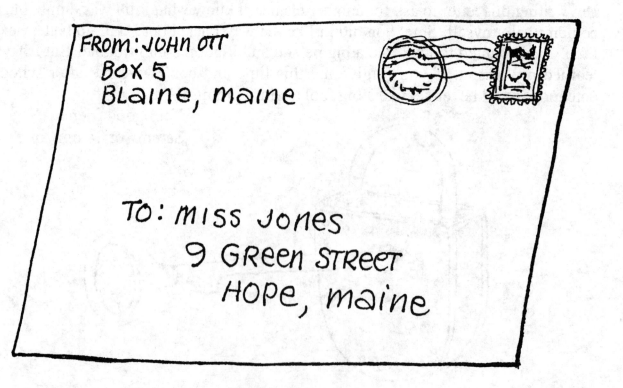

GA1513

Palindrome

A palindrome is a number or a word or a saying that reads the same backward as it does forward. The date 1881 is a palindrome. No matter how many words you know, or how many words you can spell, if you were asked to give an example of a palindrome you would probably have some trouble. Instead, it may be more rewarding for a beginning effort to see if you can pick out palindromes in the phrases and sentences that follow.

Single-Word Palindromes:

- Say, ma'm, that's a cute pup.
- Wow! I did it again.
- King Tut had one brown eye.
- Dad adjourned the meeting at noon.
- Hannah and her son Otto have a radar machine.
- Eve, please put aside the baby's bib and come hold this level.
- You call it pop but I call it soda.
- If you toot your own horn for doing a good deed, you are a dud.
- If I hear another peep out of you, I will put a gag over your mouth.

Full-Sentence Palindromes:

- Madam, I'm Adam.
- Was it a bar or a bat I saw?
- No, it is open on one position.
- Poor Dan is in a droop.

madam, I'm Adam.

GA1513

Pantoum Poem

A pantoum is a Malayan poetic form invented in the fifteenth century. When it was popularized later, it became a poem of "indefinite" length, which uses each line twice. Each stanza has four lines. The first line of the poem is the last. The fascination of this form is that it has the quality of a puzzle whose parts appear and reappear to form an intriguing tapestry of words. The writer may change original lines if they do not seem to work well when they are repeated later in the body of the poem.

Nonrhyming verse works the best. Take your time and keep trying until you determine that the final poem is the way you want it to be. As you look at the pantoum poem on the next page, "I Hate Change," you will see that the lines are numbered.

The repetition starts in the second stanza on line 5 where you use line 2 above; on line 7 you use line 4 above; on line 9 you use line 6 above and so forth until you have worked down to line 28 where you use the first line of the poem and thereby have finished your poem.

GA1513

I Hate Change*
A Pantoum

1	Don't tell me what I cannot bear
2	All things and people change
3	Some feel, in this, no loss at all
4	For me there's desperate pain.
5-2	All things and people change
6	No, nothing stays the same
7-4	For me there's desperate pain
8	It rends my soul to face.
9-6	No, nothing stays the same
10	The earth beneath me shifts
11-8	It rends my soul to face
12	The cruelty of change.
13-10	The earth beneath me shifts
14	As distant voices fade
15-12	The cruelty of change
16	Sweet laughter falls away.
17-14	As distant voices fade
18	Where will the faces go
19-16	Sweet laughter falls away
20	No memory is safe.
21-18	Where will the faces go
22	I yearn to hold them close
23-20	No memory is safe
24	Will life just fade away?
25-22	I yearn to hold them close
26	On evanescent air
27-24	Will life just fade away?
28-1	Don't tell me what I cannot bear.

Greta B. Lipson

---

* *Audacious Poetry* (GA1417), by Greta B. Lipson, © 1992, Good Apple, Carthage, Illinois.

GA1513

Paper Bodies

Though everyone in the world has a face and eyes and nose and mouth and hair, we are all, incredibly, a unique piece of work. Imagine an upcoming open house or an anticipated special event when the class members want to demonstrate to the parents or the school at large that each student is one of a kind. Or perhaps you are simply having an ordinary day that needs an imaginative inspiration to spark the atmosphere! This is the perfect project to put on display which requires everybody's humor and best effort.

Directions:

1. Cut a piece of white butcher paper to the exact height of each person in the class.
2. Each student will lie down on the paper so that a partner can trace the body of the subject.
3. The paper body will be given all the facial and body features including garments. Use magic markers, crayons, paint, or whatever is practical.
4. Identify the subject by name and write a brief autobiography on the paper body if you like.

These life-size bodies can be pasted up on the wall, draped over desks, hung, or stacked. There is something wonderfully eerie about the finished product.

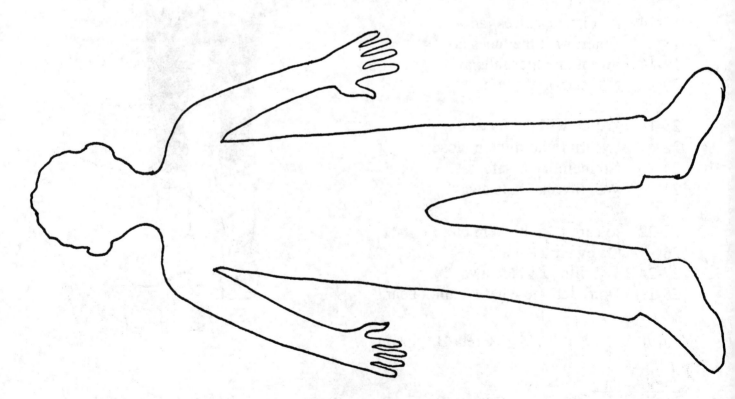

Personal Change

When we look back on some of the things we did as very young children, it is hard to believe that we were so different than we are now. Tap your memory and record some of the things you formerly did. What ideas did you have as a youngster which have changed greatly? Make a "Then and Now" list. Contrast those actions and attitudes you had as a little kid with your current and more mature style. How long is your list and how much do you remember? What are some of those startling changes in your development?

Then: When I was little I could hardly stay on my bike without my brother's help.
Now: I am looking forward to driver's training in a real car!

Then: When I was little I wanted to go everywhere my sister went.
Now: I have my own friends and wouldn't be caught dead with hers.

Then: Halloween frightened me half to death.
Now: I won a prize for the most frightening costume at our block party.

Then: My night-light had to be on all night.
Now: I enjoy listening to music when the room is pitch black.

Then: It was impossible for me to catch a ball.
Now: I am the catcher on the Baseball All-Stars at school.

GA1513

Political Cartoon

Teacher:

If you ever wanted evidence that comprehension depends upon prior knowledge, a student analysis of a political cartoon can prove the point vividly! For my first experience with this lesson I used an editorial cartoon that was simple and straightforward. I duplicated the cartoon for study partners to examine and discuss.

The big question was: What do you see and what does it mean? The students were to interpret every single item in the cartoon. Roughly described: At the top was the banner "Other Voices." On the bottom it read, "The making of the President." There was a 1984 date, with a source at the bottom which established legal copyright and ownership by a company. The cartoon consisted of a large shadow of Mickey Mouse and a complicated television camera. It was produced during an election year.

Some of the students did not recognize the television camera. Those who did understood the election to be a true media event with all the hoopla that goes with it. Mickey Mouse was familiar to all and suggested that the election took on comic proportions. The reader had to bring a degree of sophistication and prior knowledge to this seemingly simple cartoon in order to understand all of its content and its intent. On the following page are questions which can be used for other political cartoons.

GA1513

Questions to Address on the Chalkboard

Adapt these for the class.

1. What do you see in this cartoon (literal explanation)?
2. What do you infer from the cartoon? What does the artist imply?
3. What has your experience to do with the concepts involved?
4. What concepts are implicit or explicit?
5. How then do these concepts relate to comprehension, perception, agreement, or disagreement?
6. Does an editorial cartoon represent truth or opinion? Explain.
7. What is the difference between fact or opinion? State a fact about any subject. State an opinion about the same subject.
8. Cut out political cartoons over a period of weeks. Mount these on construction paper with a student comment under each cartoon for display.

GA1513

Positive Profile

Each student will fold a piece of construction paper with a personal snapshot on the cover. The following form is to be filled out and stapled inside the folder.

My complete name is _____

My nickname is _____

My favorite school subject is _____

My strong characteristic is _____

_____

_____

_____

Something I need to work on is _____

My hobby is _____

The smartest thing I ever did was _____

_____

_____

_____

The dumbest thing I ever did was _____

_____

_____

_____

I would like to be known as _____

_____

After school I enjoy _____

_____

A piece of clothing I am crazy about is _____

_____

My parents think that _____

_____

_____

When I am an adult I would like to have a career as _____

_____

The most important event in my life was _____

_____

_____

I look forward to _____

_____

An adult I admire is _____

The greatest compliment I ever received was from_____

_____

_____

Three positive statements about me from a friend, a teacher, a teammate, parent, or
other person of choice:

- _____

  _____

  _____

- _____

  _____

  _____

- _____

  _____

  _____

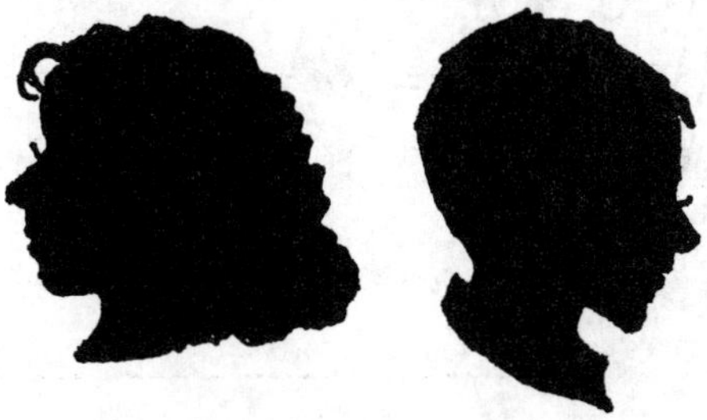

GA1513

Primary Pen Pals

Have you ever considered the pleasure of being a pen pal for a first or second grader? If you were to assume such a role there would be so much that you could offer a primary pupil! You could exchange letters and cards, which you would design yourself, during special event times. In this way you could try to create a new and purposeful interest in reading for your primary grade correspondent. The little ones would, of course, write or draw greetings to send back to you!

Both your teacher and theirs could cooperate in the planning to organize a smooth effort. Names would be assigned so that everyone would have a partner and could participate fully in the correspondence. Consider the following as suggested special days and times to launch and sustain this Pen Pal Project:

Any Month: Hello, New Friend
October: Halloween
November: Thanksgiving
December: Winter Holidays
January: New Year's
February: Groundhog Day, Valentine's Day
March: St. Patrick's Day, Kite Festivals
April: April Fools' Day, Easter Rabbits, Arbor Day, Earth Day
May: May Day, Mother's Day, Cinco de Mayo
June: Flag Day, Official Summer, Father's Day

GA1513

Reporter at Large*

Imagine opening up your daily paper and finding newspaper accounts of an old tale as if it had happened today! It is your job as a student newspaper reporter to take a look at one or more events in folklore and report on this in the daily paper where you are employed. You are a journalist who is writing copy for any section of the daily paper from headlines to classified ads. Include as many sections of the daily paper as you can. To demonstrate the possibilities, list some familiar books or fairy tales on the chalkboard. Here are some examples.

The Wall Street Kernel

- Headline: Goldilocks charged by police with breaking and entering. Mr. & Mrs. Burly Bear outraged with brazen blonde.

- Business Section: "The Goose That Laid the Golden Egg." Wall Street reports gold prices rise after Goosie was put on the chopping block. No more easy money for foolish Farmer!

- Society Section: "The Frog Prince" The impertinent Prince Greenspan is regarded as a social climber by many in the castle. It is rumored that he is from the lowly swamp kingdom of Amphibia and is determined to obtain a legal green card.

- Obituary: "Giant, Hugh Mungus." Age 50. Victim of assault by Jack, a local vengeful youth. Mr. Mungus was thought to have been a pituitary giant who suffered considerable pain and estrangement as a child. His death is hailed by some citizens. Others believe his civil rights were violated. The family asks that, in lieu of flowers, contributions be sent to The Center for the Study of Civil Peace.

- Advertisement: Did the Pied Piper spirit your child away? Are you desperately lonely in your childless home? Fill your home and your heart again with a "Rent a Kid." Call our unique service. Reasonable rates. No deal refused from Hamelin residents. Bring in this ad!

GA1513

- Editorial: There has been a systematic breakdown of discipline in the schools as demonstrated by the recent disgrace of Mary's lamb following her to Woolcott Elementary yesterday! Because the lamb was permitted to stay until dismissal, the Board of Education promises immediate disciplinary measures! Who is at fault?

GOLDILOCKS CHARGED

LONELY?? TOO QUIET at YOUR HOUSE??
RENT-A-KID!!
REASONABLE RATES
CALL 1-800-222-AKID
!!NO DEal REFUSED!!

LAMB COMES TO SCHOOL (AP) Mary forgot to close the gate when she left home yesterday morning. Her pet lamb followed her to school.

A memorial has been established for the center for the Study of Civil Peace.

---

* *The Scoop on Frogs and Princes*, by Greta B. Lipson and Eric B. Lipson, Good Apple © 1993, Carthage, Illinois.

 # Revolt of the Machines

In the poem "Nightmare Number Three" by Stephen Vincent Benet (1896-1943), the poet describes the horrors of a society in which the machines rise in a ruthless revolt against humans.

This strange circumstance is a theme which has been explored before by numerous writers. Many people who have had a bad day with a toaster, the computer, an elevator, or a breakdown of the family car begin to feel that all of this mechanical failure is a conspiracy by the machines to assert their power over our lives.

Imagine if the technology upon which we depend so heavily would begin to act as if there were a decision to take over humans! Write a description of such a harrowing event. Read your descriptions aloud and share the nightmare. Follow up this written exercise by reading Stephen Vincent Benet's poem in the collection *Modern American Poetry**. Nothing can match the experience of reading the original account.

A report of the incident, expressed by a citizen who experienced the uprising, follows.

****

Terror in the Business Section

We never expected revolt.
But one does wonder when they started thinking–
Perhaps it was a plan that started years ago.
If you think about it maybe the clues were all there, but we didn't pay attention.
In a recent accident it appeared as if a concrete mixer had actually eaten a man–but
  who would believe that?
This plan had to have been the work of the super machines, the ones that
  demonstrated almost human skills.
Then there were the cars that came after us like hunters.
Maybe they became wildly angry and came to despise the smell of us and our
  hands.

GA1513

There were such awful shocks in store, like in the office where a worker was
    strangled in a maze of telephone wires which continued to weave in defiance
    over his head.
In one building after another we climbed stairs breathlessly, afraid to ride the
    elevators.
We gave them the capacity to think, and there's evidence of that.
We built them and taught them—so maybe, like humans, they may be willing to
    compromise with us.
The only thing that bothers me is what are they going to eat.
I've seen some signs of blood—
Maybe I was mistaken.

* "Nightmare Number Three," by Stephen Vincent Benet, © 1927, originally in
Selected Works of Stephen Vincent Benet, Rinehart & Co. Later appeared in
Modern American Poetry, published by Harcourt, Brace & Jovanovich, © 1962,
edited by Louis Untermeyer.

90

Rip Van Winkle

American folklore is enriched by the works of the author Washington Irving (1783-1859) who wrote "Rip Van Winkle." This charming character comes to life in Irving's book of folklore entitled *The Sketch Book*. Rip is a cheerful ne'er-do-well, encountered in the mountains where he lives. Rip carouses with a band of dwarves; and after some heavy drinking and a vigorous game of bowling, he falls fast asleep. He sleeps soundly for twenty long years and awakens to find that his entire world has changed. His wife has passed away, his daughter is married, and he has slept through the entire American Revolution! The residents of his town think he is an old man who has quite lost his mind until he is recognized by a former neighbor.

This strange occurrence has been reenacted, in some ways, by a modern day Rip. In 1991 Sergei Krikalev, a Russian cosmonaut, was sent into space where he stayed on the Mir Space Station for ten months. He returned home in March 1992 to find that the USSR–the country which he left–was no longer in existence. The communist government had fallen, and even the name of his hometown of Leningrad had been changed to St. Petersburg. He seemed to be in good health, but he said that being back on the ground of his own planet was literally making him a little dizzy! Given such circumstances, anyone would feel dizzy.

Imagine that the same kind of event has occurred to you. Like Rip, you have arrived back home after a twenty-year interlude only to find incredible changes in your hometown, your country, and everyone you know. Describe your experience, and include information about the changes in your family.

GA1513

Rules of the Room

Conventional wisdom holds that rules in the classroom should be made democratically whenever possible. It is easier to respect rules when the reason for each is clearly defined. Since rules are guidelines for the good of the group, some rules, in time, may be eliminated or modified to fit the circumstances. The aim of posting rules is to sensitize everyone to the ways in which daily life is managed in school.

With the teacher in the role of the final decision maker, the class may begin to list the rules which everyone thinks may help smooth the operation of the classroom. When the most comprehensive list is organized, illustrate the rules with humor to make them emphatic and give them zing. This serious business can provide more than a few good laughs at the hands of class members!

NO PAPER SCRUNCHING

GA1513

Runonsentence

If you have ever wondered why we use punctuation, the following story makes it very clear! In ancient times monks and religious scribes established a system of punctuation in manuscripts so the written word could be more easily read. Without spacings, markings and separations, printed material is not only miserable to read, but even the meaning can be obscured! Try your patience with the words below. Put in the periods and capitals. Eliminate conjunctions ("and, but, because . . .") and then you will be able to unlock the story. Do you believe the events actually happened? Do you believe it was a psychological trick? What do you think? Can you read it aloud?

WellthetruthisInevereverwantedtodohomeworkandnobodycouldfindasol
utiontomyproblembutonedaymygrandfatherinvitedmetogointomyrooma
ndheassuredmethatonthatdaymylifewouldbechangedbecausehetoldmehe
hadfiguredoutawaytokeepmeinthereuntilIactuallyfinishedmyhomework
wellIdidn'tbelievehimbutIwentalongwithhimbecausehe'saswelloldguyan
dIknowheworriesaboutmebeingsuchalazyslugwithschoolworkIsatdownn
icelyandstartedonmyworkbutasusualinashorttimeIcouldfeelthatoldimpul
setogetupandleavemyschoolworkforlatersoIwalkedovertothedoorandcon
gratulatedmyselfonhoweasythiswasifmygrandfatherthoughthehadamagic
solutionformehewascertainlymistakenjustasIturnedthehandleofthedoorIh
eardalowanimalrumblethatmademyheartbeatsofastIthoughtIwouldfaintI
waitedafewminutesandputmyhandontheknobandonceagainthatrumbleca
merollingoutofachestwhichmusthavebelongedtoahugecreatureprobablya
bearasIlistenedwithmyearagainstthedoorthesoundofbeastlybreathingcam
einasteadyrhythmwhenIventuredclosertothedoortherewasaninstantgrowl

     GA1513

ingasifthecreaturecouldsmellmypresenceIcannottellyouhowterrifiedIwas

Iwasafraidtocalltoanyoneforfearthatpowerfulcreaturewouldbecomeenrag

edwithmeandbetemptedtoteardownthedoordutifullyItiptoedbacktothetabl

eandsatdowntheclocktickedslowlyslowlyasIappliedmyselftothemiserable

taskofhomeworkwhenIfinishedIwalkedtothedoorstillterrifiedthatontheot

hersidewasamonstrousanimalthatwouldtearmetopiecesIwasverycautious

andsweatingasIapproachednosoundcamefromtheothersideItriedthedoork

nobturningitinslowmotionasmystomachdidsomersaultsbuttherewasonlys

ilenceIheldmybreathandtookawildchanceasIopenedthatdoorandfoundabs

olutelynothingIcouldn'tbelievemygrandfatherwouldpullsuchatreacherou

sstuntonmebutIwasn'ttakinganychancesasIleftthebedroomIheldmyfinish

edhomeworkovermyheadlikeasoldiersurrenderingtotheotherside!

Translation:

Well the truth is I never, ever wanted to do homework and nobody could find a solution to my problem. One day my grandfather invited me to go into my room, and he assured me that on that day my life would be changed. He told me he had figured out a way to keep me in there until I actually finished my homework. Well, I didn't believe him, but I went along with him because he's a swell old guy, and I know he worries about me being such a lazy slug with schoolwork!

I sat down nicely and started on my work but as usual, in a short time, I could feel that old impulse to get up and leave my schoolwork for later. I walked over to the door and congratulated myself on how easy this was. If my grandfather thought he had a magic solution for me, he was certainly mistaken. Just as I turned the handle of the door, I heard a low animal rumble that made my heart beat so fast, I thought I would faint! I waited a few minutes and put my hand on the knob and once again that rumble came rolling out of a chest which must have belonged to a huge creature, probably a bear! As I listened with my ear against the door, the sound of beastly breathing came in a steady rhythm. When I ventured closer to the door, there was an instant growling as if the creature could smell my presence. I cannot tell you how terrified I was. I was afraid to call to anyone for fear that powerful creature would become enraged with me and be tempted to tear down the door.

GA1513

Dutifully I tiptoed back to the table and sat down. The clock ticked slowly, slowly, as I applied myself to the miserable task of homework. When I finished I walked to the door still terrified that on the other side was a monstrous animal that would tear me to pieces! I was very cautious and sweating. As I approached, no sound came from the other side. I tried the doorknob, turning it in slow motion as my stomach did somersaults, but there was only silence. I held my breath and took a wild chance as I opened that door and found absolutely nothing. I couldn't believe my grandfather would pull such a treacherous stunt on me, but I wasn't taking any chances. As I left the bedroom I held my finished homework over my head like a soldier surrendering to the other side.

GA1513

Scavenger Hunt

This story is hard to believe, but it is absolutely true. In 1979 an extraordinary picture book was published in England. It was called *Masquerade* and was written by Kit Williams, who was also the illustrator of the book. It was clear from the beginning that the book was for all ages, but it was the adults in England who went wild over it because it held the secret of a buried treasure which could be found "somewhere in the British Isles."

First, Williams had the treasure custom-made. It was a $6000 jeweled rabbit pendant set with turquoise, moonstones, and rubies. Then he actually buried it. In his picture book *Masquerade*, Williams included oblique clues on every page to tantalize or help searchers find the precious necklace. It was also necessary for the searchers to have some acquaintance with historical facts as well, in order to unlock some of the evidence. Searchers hunted unsuccessfully for three years; even people from far-off countries arrived to dig holes all over England in their frantic quest for the necklace.

A design engineer, who finally found the necklace, had become so frenzied that he had quit the search many times. He had decided at one point that he had to control his passion to find the treasure because the hunt was beginning to rule his life. It was not so much the piece of jewelry that mattered to him–it was the challenge of the quest! More than once he broke his shovel and threw up his hands in surrender, but still the unremitting passion persisted.

One memorable day, this determined man (with the assumed name of "Ken Thomas") took his dog out for a walk in the park to do the things that dogs must do. And indeed, of all the rocks on which the dog could attend to business he chose the very one that revealed the secret of *Masquerade*. The last clue to the jeweled pendant led Ken to its hiding place in a Bedfordshire village thirty-five miles north of London. In three years the rabbit pendant had increased in price from $6000 to $36,000.

Your Scavenger Hunt

- The first task you have is to find the book *Masquerade: The Complete Book with the Answers Explained* by Kit Williams (Workman Publishing, New York, 1983) so that all the class members can read it and discover for themselves just how mysterious the clues to the scavenger hunt were.

- The next task is to organize the class into four or five working groups. Each group will get together and design a cunning plan for a scavenger hunt that is safe, challenging, clever, and involves items which can be brought from home to school. When all the plans are handed in, the teacher will decide which one is the most unique.

- A panel of judges or monitors will be the guardians of the rules of the hunt. In the event that a final decision must be made, the panel's judgment will prevail.

- The rules of the hunt are up to the class to decide. Will there be an incentive, a prize, or just the recognition of having been incredibly smart?

GA1513

Scrambled Cities

If you rearrange all the letters in a word, you have created an anagram. Look at a map of the world and select the names of some major cities. Write the names and look at them carefully. How many of these names can you rearrange so that they are still *pronounceable*? Is there more than one spelling variation for a single city? How many can be unscrambled by other readers? First write out the city and include the state or province before transposing the letters. Here are some examples of city anagrams:

Tucson (Arizona) Conuts
New York (New York) Kron Yew
Dallas (Texas) Sallad
Winnipeg (Manitoba) Gipniwen
Boston (Massachusetts) Bonots
Detroit (Michigan) Trodiet
Raleigh, (N. C.) Leg Hair
Aspen (Colorado) Pensa
Chicago (Illinois) Gachico
St. Paul (Minnesota) Salt up
Toronto (Ontario) Rottoon

For a really difficult anagram, try some longer names, such as San Francisco, Los Angeles, Minneapolis, or Tallahassee.

Compare your answers to others in the class by reviewing the list of names above. Record the spelling variations on the chalkboard. Any contribution may be challenged if it appears that someone has left out a letter, transposed incorrectly, or used too many letters. What scrambled cities are the most innovative or the funniest?

Sibling Status

Parents Are Confusing

You're too old for this,
You're too young for that.
It's conflicting, confusing—
A dangerous trap!

Be a mother to your sister,
Be a sister to your brother,
Be a warm and loving person
To a multitude of others.

Get your elbows off the table.
Keep your footsies on the floor.
Finish food that's on your platter
Before you ask for more.

Don't interrupt a speaker.
Never contradict a parent.
Don't give the bad impression
That your manners are quite errant.

Always tell the truth,
But hurting feelings is forbidden.
Be honest and revealing,
But white lies will be forgiven.

Be sensible when making friends.
Screen out the saints and sinners.
(The trouble is, we don't agree
On which friends are the winners!)

The list of rules goes on at length
And so it will behoove you
To try your best to understand
So then we can improve you!

Greta B. Lipson

GA1513

Sibling Status

I am the oldest ____ youngest ____ middle ____ only child ____

I have problems because _____

My mother's attitude is _____

My father's attitude is _____

I know that we all have problems. For example:

Younger kids always _____

Middle kids always _____

Older kids always _____

****

• Divide into groups and plan "role reversal" skits to present to the class. Decide on a single problem or source of conflict between adults and teens. One of you will be the parent and one will be the teenager. In a five-minute skit, try to get to the heart of the problem as each person makes his or her position clear. Discuss what you observed during each skit. Is right or wrong easily defined, or does it depend upon point of view? Did you change your mind about any issue? Did anything that was said give you more understanding?

• Based upon the poem "Parents Are Confusing," your personal experience, and the skit, what advice could you give to involved adults?

100

GA1513

Silent Bugaboos

One of the problems in the spelling, writing, and reading of the English language has to do with the different sounds of many spelling combinations. The famous Irish playwright and critic George Bernard Shaw (1856-1950) was a leader in the movement to change English spelling to a phonetic system.

In order to demonstrate the contradictions and confusion in our spelling, he came up with the word *ghoti* to make the point that we have many different sounds for the same letters and letter combinations.

Examine the word *ghoti*. What word do you think it spells? Think of the following letter combinations which sound differently in other words considering our unphonetic system.

> Answer: Think of "gh" as it sounds in "enough"
> Think of "o" as it sounds in "women"
> Think of "ti" as it sounds in "nation"
> The word is "FISH"

- Can you do something similar?
- If George Bernard Shaw were alive today and you were determined to help him, how many spelling words could you change to support the cause of phonetic spelling? Try these: *bread, thumb, science, edge, steak, phone, salmon, night, psychology, physics, island, soldier, knight, colonel, answer, Tuesday, laugh, height.*
- How would phonetic "basic spelling" make writing easier for you?

I'LL HAVE YOU KNOW YOU MUST BEHAVE.

GA1513

Sloppy Sign Painter

In your summer travels you pass through the little town of GOTCHL–a place of historical importance which you have always wanted to visit. All your friends have told you that you would experience the adventure of a lifetime if you spent some time in this quaint village. They said, "Just wander around as a typical tourist, ask lots of questions, and enjoy yourself. But, make sure you see the sights with a reliable tour book in hand."

Things go all right for a while until you try to read the local signs, and that's when the trouble begins! Can these signs be written in English you wonder? What seems to be the trouble?

WHEN I STOQQED to GeT GUS in GOTCHL, I TOOK a WRONG TURT and enDeD UP in a TUNNeF, WHICH LeD to a SHaRP CaRVe RIGHT in FRONT of a MeTeL and ReSTaPRaNT.

WELCOME TO THE VILLAGE OF GOTCHL
QUEST (GUEST)
GUS (GAS)
STOQ (STOP)
TURT (TURN)
WALZ (WALK)
EFIT (EXIT)
TUNNEF (TUNNEL)
NO SOOKING (NO SMOKING)
SMOULDER (SHOULDER)
CRESSING (CROSSING)
RESTAPRANT (RESTAURANT)
TOILER (TOILET)
METEL (MOTEL)
CARVE (CURVE)
DAGGER (DANGER)
BRIGGE (BRIDGE)

Finally you begin to see a pattern in the signs. If you change one letter in the sign it will make sense. By the way, the sign painter pulled the same sloppy trick when painting the name of the town. Change the final "L" to "A" and what do you have?

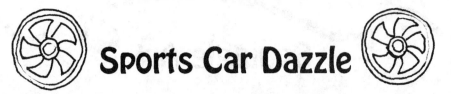

Sports Car Dazzle

Automobiles are a big business in our country because we practically live on wheels. There are many automotive consulting firms, marketing and engineering experts, and automotive publications which review cars such as *Car and Driver, Road and Track, Motor Trend, Autoweek,* and *Automobile Magazine* to name a few. Daily newspapers also feature car reviews and activities for car buffs. There is something for everybody in the marketplace, from the folks who love antique cars to those who follow the brand-new models.

One special breed of car owners is those who love sleek sports cars. The names selected for cars of all types are very important. Just the right name is a flashy lure that is intended to catch the attention of a particular customer. Assume that you are a member of a marketing team working on a name for a new sports car which is almost ready to hit the showrooms. All of you have reviewed some of the names of cars presently available which are:

- Acura NSX
- Mercedes-Benz SL Series
- Nissan 300 ZX
- Porsche 911
- Mazda RX7
- Dodge Stealth
- Chevrolet Corvette

Work in a group to find just the right name for your particular sports car. Look up the meaning of the word *evoke* in the context of your company's assignment. When you select the car's perfect name, what feeling do you want to "evoke" in the people you hope will become your customers? How would your team describe this hot new model? Draw a picture of this dream car on another sheet of paper.

Squiggle Art

If you have had the privilege of going to an art museum and have spent hours looking at the paintings hanging on the walls, or if you have looked at a book of paintings, you will recall that some paintings are representational–the images are recognizable. This "traditional" art captures people and their environment almost as we see them in real life.

Other paintings may be "abstract" art, in which we see a different artistic approach to the use of colors and forms. The subjects we see in abstract art do not resemble images we recognize in real life. Either way, we are looking at artistic expression.

In this plan for squiggle art, each student will start with a piece of manila drawing paper on which a bold stroke is made in the middle of the paper with magic marker. The paper is then passed to a different student who proceeds to incorporate that stroke into a full-scale piece of representational or abstract art.

Each paper must have the name of the initiator and the name of the final artist. The picture must be given an appropriate title, as all pictures have, to give a clue to the subject matter, such as "Dog on a Skateboard," "Pizza Suspended on a Chandelier," "Female Slam-Dunk Star," "Sunrise over Lake Okeechobee," "Nausea on a Roller Coaster."

The pictures may be executed with any medium the class members prefer such as crayons, paints, markers, pastels, torn paper, or any other workable materials. Exhibit the pictures. Artists may be called upon to explain their artistry.

Include the art teacher in this project for an inter-curricular plan.

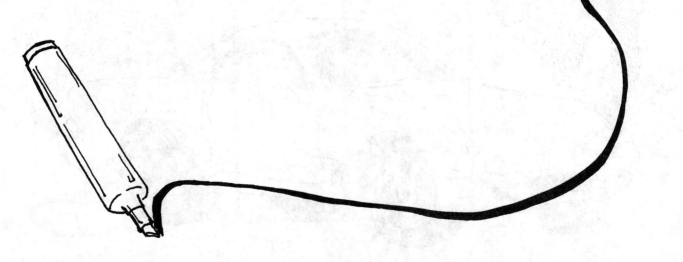

GA1513

Stained-Glass Window

One of the most impressive enhancements of churches, temples, universities, libraries, and museums is the exquisite addition of stained-glass windows. This highly specialized art has been developing since the year 1000 and continues to strike a sense of awe and deep appreciation in the eyes of the viewer. The windows evoke a feeling of ethereal art because of the play of light that comes through the multicolored glass, casting airy, heavenly rays!

The construction of these windows is very complex since they are made up of many pieces and thicknesses of colored glass. The divisions between the pieces of glass, which are leaded together, must be in just the right proportion without too much clutter. The way in which the light hits the window is another factor for the artist to consider, as well as the position of the people who admire this piece of art.

The rough draft of the window, produced by the artist in the planning period, is called a cartoon–a name which may sound inappropriate, given the heavenly qualities of the finished work. But this does suggest that with paper, pencil, paint, magic markers, crayons, colored paper, tinted cellophane and more, you, too, may be able to create a stained-glass window. If there is an art resource teacher in your school, he or she may be able to contribute special skills and suggestions for such a project. A compass may be a productive and interesting tool to use for this drawing as well. See the outline of the windows below.

States and Capitals

Organize into teams for a "speak out" exercise. Each team member will receive a reproduced copy of alphabetized states in the United States. A second page will have the capitals and state abbreviations. Take your turn as each team tries to match up the capitals with the states and their abbreviations. As an ongoing exercise, any variation of the game that is a challenge is acceptable!

Capitals	Abbreviations	States
MONTGOMERY	AL	ALABAMA
JUNEAU	AK	ALASKA
PHOENIX	AZ	ARIZONA
LITTLE ROCK	AR	ARKANSAS
SACRAMENTO	CA	CALIFORNIA
DENVER	CO	COLORADO
HARTFORD	CT	CONNECTICUT
DOVER	DE	DELAWARE
TALLAHASSEE	FL	FLORIDA
ATLANTA	GA	GEORGIA
HONOLULU	HI	HAWAII
BOISE	ID	IDAHO
SPRINGFIELD	IL	ILLINOIS
INDIANAPOLIS	IN	INDIANA
DES MOINES	IA	IOWA
TOPEKA	KS	KANSAS
FRANKFORT	KY	KENTUCKY
BATON ROUGE	LA	LOUISIANA
AUGUSTA	ME	MAINE
ANNAPOLIS	MD	MARYLAND
BOSTON	MA	MASSACHUSETTS
LANSING	MI	MICHIGAN
ST. PAUL	MN	MINNESOTA
JACKSON	MS	MISSISSIPPI
JEFFERSON CITY	MO	MISSOURI
HELENA	MT	MONTANA
LINCOLN	NE	NEBRASKA
CARSON CITY	NV	NEVADA
CONCORD	NH	NEW HAMPSHIRE
TRENTON	NJ	NEW JERSEY
SANTA FE	NM	NEW MEXICO
ALBANY	NY	NEW YORK
RALEIGH	NC	NORTH CAROLINA
BISMARCK	ND	NORTH DAKOTA
COLUMBUS	OH	OHIO
OKLAHOMA CITY	OK	OKLAHOMA
SALEM	OR	OREGON
HARRISBURG	PA	PENNSYLVANIA
PROVIDENCE	RI	RHODE ISLAND
COLUMBIA	SC	SOUTH CAROLINA
PIERRE	SD	SOUTH DAKOTA
NASHVILLE	TN	TENNESSEE
AUSTIN	TX	TEXAS
SALT LAKE CITY	UT	UTAH
MONTPELIER	VT	VERMONT
RICHMOND	VA	VIRGINIA
OLYMPIA	WA	WASHINGTON
CHARLESTON	WV	WEST VIRGINIA
MADISON	WI	WISCONSIN
CHEYENNE	WY	WYOMING

GA1513

Teen Speak

Teenagers use slang as a way of excluding outsiders and establishing their own separate unique character. All language is a dynamic form which responds to cultural growth and change, but the fastest changing language is always the faddish forms adopted by young people. New expressions appear quickly and may disappear just as quickly, but everyone belonging to the "in-group" understands what the new vocabulary means. How many current words or phrases can you list? How many can you define? Ask an adult in school or at home for some very old slang with definitions. Use the information for an old timer's list.

Teen Speak*

Like dude
Like man
Like find the meaning if you can
She goes
He goes
Translate it if you understand

Ya know, ya know
Ya know in every phrase
For sure,
Ya know
We hear it every place.

You're bad
You're good
Now get out of my face!

So lighten up
And cool it spaz
You're awesome and unreal
If you can't figure all this out
Don't make it such a deal.

Pretend that you are not a dweeb,
A simp, a wimp, or nerd
Just listen up the best you can
To every far-out word

It's context that'll clue you in
To the hippest of locutions
Just groove it, move it, all around
And reach your own conclusions.
                    Greta B. Lipson

---

* *Audacious Poetry* (GA1417) by Greta B. Lipson, © 1992, Good Apple, Carthage, Illinois.

GA1513

Time Travel

If you could travel backward in time and had the opportunity to start all over again, how would you change things? Sometimes people say they would like to go back in time but only if they could be as smart as they are now. Otherwise, they say, what is the point of a new beginning if you do the same foolish things all over again?

Think of this as having the opportunity to do something you failed to do, or the chance to make a different choice, or being able to undo a hurtful conversation that you regretted later. The big question is: What would you change or do differently if you could go back in time? How far back in your life would you choose to travel?

If you were granted the power to change history, in what period would you travel backward and what great or wrenching event would you attempt to alter? How do you think it could be done?

And then there is a different experience to contemplate, as described by the English author H.G. Wells who in 1895 wrote the science fiction novel *The Time Machine*. In this story the inventor of the machine is able to transport himself into the future where he witnesses shocking changes in our civilization. What choice would you make for time travel? Would you go backward or into the future? Explain.

Titles to Tickle

On occasion you may see a catchy phrase in the newspaper or read a book title or notice a movie marquee with an especially intriguing ring to it. Instantly you have a reaction to it and wonder what it's all about.

Well, this is your lucky day! Starting with the list below, the teacher will read each item on the list slowly and point to someone in the room to elicit a quick response. The person selected must immediately express an impression, a remark, or a question which is prompted by the title. If there is no answer, another student may volunteer an answer. Expand the list by adding interesting contributions from class members which will generate sure-fire reactions.

For example:
- Dirke the Dogman (He's got a problem.)
- Cheeseburger Heaven (A sweet place to be)
- Slam Dunk Capers (Basketball mania)
- Jack, the Computer Hack (A brilliant criminal)
- Tales of a Baseball Clown (Goofy mascot)
- Pepperoni Pals (Let's tackle a pizza.)
- Football Fantasies (Girls on the gridiron)
- The Skeleton's Secret (Murder most foul)
- Tillie Trunsky, Private Eye (Brains, not brawn)
- The Thief Who Ate Too Much
  (Caught by calories)
- Teen Troubles (A bad hair day)
- Ghost Freighter (Mutiny on the high seas)

GA1513

Triolet

A triolet is a poem or stanza having eight lines of eight syllables each. Line one is repeated in lines four and seven. The second line is repeated in line eight. The rhyme scheme is abaaabab. Study the following example.

Parental Triolet*

	1. Being with parents isn't cool. a
	2. It's just because it looks all wrong. b
	3. It's very much a rigid rule. a
(repeat line 1)	4. Being with parents isn't cool. a
	5. Don't want to look like little fools! a
	6. With folks is not where we belong. b
(repeat line 1)	7. Being with parents isn't cool. a
(repeat line 2)	8. It's just because it looks all wrong. b

Greta B. Lipson

Try your skill at writing a triolet. Think of a topic which interests you and which has possibilities for rhyme. When examining the rhyme scheme above, you will see that there are only two words which are the basis for rhymes: *cool* and the words with which it rhymes and *wrong* and the words with which it rhymes. Numbering the lines will also help with the construction. In counting eight syllables use your fingers and your ears!

* *Audacious Poetry* (GA1417), by Greta B. Lipson, © 1992, Good Apple, Carthage, Illinois.

Useful Things

Have you ever wondered about the countless little things that make daily living easier? How did it happen that pencils, forks, spoons, zippers, paper clips, cellophane tape, staples, can openers, ballpoint pens, cleansing tissues, and soap were invented? Certainly we feel we couldn't live without these convenient items. But what creative minds germinated the ideas? How were the inventions marketed?

The stories behind these inventions are fascinating as is the history of the shopping cart invented in 1937 by Sylvan Goldman, a grocer in Oklahoma. He observed that his customers were lugging around hand-held baskets that were heavy and cumbersome. He reasoned that putting wheels on the baskets would be easier and would encourage more purchases; but people, set in their ways, ignored the carts he placed in the store for their convenience.

Not easily discouraged, Mr. Goldman, a funny and innovative businessman, hired people to come in and act as if they were customers as they busily loaded their baskets with great quantities of groceries. The ruse worked and his real customers finally accepted shopping carts so enthusiastically that carts are currently "the most often used item on four wheels, second only to the automobile."*

Remember that when Alexander Graham Bell invented the telephone, the public attitude was that the phone was just a frivolous toy. For those people who are truly curious, an authentic research project can be a follow-up regarding even larger items such as the automobile, radio, TV, computers, and duplicating machines.

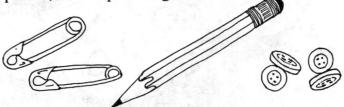

* *The Invention of Ordinary Things*, by Don L. Wulffson, © 1981, Lothrop, Lee & Shepard, N.Y.

GA1513

Given this background, use your imagination and try to speculate about how the following items came into being. Write a page of fictional information that answers these questions: What was the need for the invention? What did the inventors experience as they developed their innovations?

A Fictional Account of the History of an Invention

Some Suggestions:

- zipper
- pencil with eraser
- shoe
- stove
- refrigerator

- alarm clock
- Velcro ™
- toothpaste
- frozen food
- bed

- mirror
- book
- rubber band
- thermos bottle
- eyeglasses

112

GA1513

Utopia

We can all agree that there is no perfection in the world we live in, though we try hard to work toward an ideal society. Writers and philosophers have written about achieving a blessed place which provides a good life for all people. As long ago as 375 B.C., the Greek philosopher Plato wrote *The Republic* describing his idea of the perfect state. He considered his Republic to be the social blueprint for citizens to aspire to.

In 1516 Sir Thomas More wrote *Utopia* in which he describes his notion of a society which has no poverty or suffering. He chose the Greek word *Utopia* which translated means "no place" and has become a universal word which describes an unattainable ideal of a nonexistent place. A "utopian" came to mean anyone who wrote about or sought after the flawless society.

Another famous utopian was Samuel Butler who in 1872 published the book *Erewhon* about an imaginary island. Look at the title carefully. What trick does it contain? (Answer: The title *Erewhon* is an anagram of the word *nowhere*.)

One of the important details to note is that each utopian takes a different view of an ideal society. Plato wanted philosophers to govern at the highest level, which not many people accepted in ancient Greece, or would accept in the modern world today!

But now it's your chance to think about the good life in a place of social harmony, justice, and security for all people. Describe your vision of Utopia in a paragraph or a page. Would it be in this country or some unknown place? Share some of these compositions by reading them aloud.

GA1513

Vending Machine

Vending machines have been around for so long that we forget just how versatile they are. They not only dispense beverages, candy, nuts, gum, sandwiches, and all manner of hot and cold foods, but they also provide services such as insurance coverage in airports, shoe shines, stamps in post offices, dry cleaning, magazines and books, personal hygiene items, and money changing services!

What most of us don't know is that one of the original vending machines existed in ancient Egypt in 200 B.C.! In a holy temple in Alexandria, there was a machine of sorts that dispensed holy water to the faithful.

In America the first vending machines in 1880 offered chewing gum on train platforms, followed in 1920 by cigarette machines. About 1925, in many fancy downtown theaters, there were machines which fastened to the backs of seats and dispensed Hershey Bars™ for a nickel! Given this background, you are to design and name a vending machine for whatever you want to dispense to the public at a profit. The sky is the limit, and the invitation to your imagination is a personal challenge!

GA1513

Villanelle

A villanelle is a poetic form invented by the French poet Jean Passerat in the late 1500s. There are usually six stanzas. The first five stanzas are three lines long. The sixth stanza has four lines. The rhyme scheme is *aba* throughout the entire poem. Lines 1 and 3 are repeated according to the pattern below. In the last stanza there is a variation which is *abaa*. There are only two rhymes allowed throughout the poem. If you feel courageous, try it! It is a brain buster.

Grandparental Connection

1	My gram and grandfather offer love like no other.	a
2	Their small house for me is a port in the storm	b
3	It took me a while to enjoy and discover.	a

4	They envelop my spirit with nurturing cover	a
5	A snug and safe harbor in a place that is warm	b
6-1	My gram and grandfather offer love like no other	a

7	Their welcome is kind. I am never a bother	a
8	I can hide in their house, castaway from a storm	b
9-3	It took me a while to enjoy and discover–	a

10	They reach out the same to my father and mother.	a
11	There's a range of the parts and the roles they perform	b
12-1	My gram and grandfather offer love like no other	a

13	My spirit once failed and they helped me recover	a
14	Like a failing young bird my strength was reborn	b
15-3	It took me a while to enjoy and discover–	a

16	Their devoted support is the gift I uncovered	a
17	It is there for the family and it waits unadorned	b
18-1	My gram and grandfather offer love like no other	a
19-3	It took me a while to enjoy and discover.	a

Greta B. Lipson

* *Audacious Poetry* (GA1417), by Greta B. Lipson, © 1992, Good Apple, Carthage, Illinois.

GA1513

 # Villanelle Pattern

1 _____ a

2 _____ b

3 _____ a

4 _____ a

5 _____ b

6-1 _____ a

7 _____ a

8 _____ b

9-3 _____ a

10 _____ a

11 _____ b

12-1 _____ a

13 _____ a

14 _____ b

15-3 _____ a

16 _____ a

17 _____ b

18-1 _____ a

19-3 _____ a

Wanted Poster

In the style of the old West, design a wanted poster offering a reward. The difference between this poster and those of frontier days will be that the rewards will be offered for the capture of people with good personalities and traits that are positive! Draw the wanted "culprit" as best you can. Add variations of your choice to make the poster unique.

WANTED: Oscar the Optimist
         $1000 reward
FOR: Being upbeat and believing that every situation will always come out just fine in the end.
FAVORITE SAYING: "Every cloud has a silver lining."
DANGER: His attitude may be contagious.
LAST SEEN: At a pep rally talking to the debate team

WANTED: Jennifer the Joker
         $1500 reward
FOR: Saving the day with a funny remark after hard times in school
FAVORITE SAYING: "Laugh and the world laughs with you."
DANGER: Helps people take themselves less seriously
LAST SEEN: Surrounded by laughing students in the cafeteria

GA1513

Weaving Poems

You are going to create a nonrhyming poem by choosing four phrases from the lyrical lines below. Add the borrowed lines to the beginning, the middle, and the ending of four (or more) of your own lines. Strike any mood that suggests itself to you. In free verse, use words that have color and power and you will have woven a unique poem! You are invited to add as many lines as you wish, as long as it makes sense. Try creating more than one poem. Those who wish to volunteer may read their poems aloud. The variations in this exercise are astonishing and impressive!

- The dream was soft in pastel shades
- Unspoken gifts of loyalty
- A crescent moon threw silver dust
- The glow was from a distant shore
- Aspiring toward the luminous horizon
- Come hear the stillness of the night
- Walk the road in gentle pathways
- Be brave and straight in troubled times
- Serving others is a reason for being
- A map of honor traced for me
- We speak as one in friendship's name
- A binding strength restores us all

GA1513

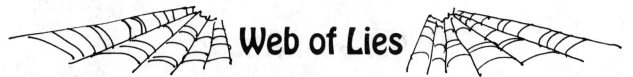

Web of Lies

Unless we are saintly, we have all had the experience of telling a lie or practicing a deception that grows more and more complex. Sir Walter Scott (1771-1832), the Scottish novelist and poet, created the hero Lochinvar who said it best: "Oh, what a tangled web we weave, when first we practice to deceive."

The metaphor of the web is so appropriate because after telling one lie it is as if one is caught in an inescapable tangle of threads. You may misspeak yourself, and then, in an attempt to make the first lie sound plausible, you are caught up in more story strands than you can possibly keep sorted out!

A classic example of this is the tragedy of Romeo Montagu who was sixteen and Juliet Capulet who was thirteen when first they met and fell in love. Because a bitter feud between the two families kept them apart, the two young people contrived an elaborate plan to stay together. Juliet was to lie to her father and pretend she would marry the young prince, Paris, whom her father had chosen for her. The downward spiral started with Juliet's deception. The cruel twists and turns of unforeseen events descended and resulted in a wave of lies and tragedy that swept Romeo and Juliet to their ill-timed deaths.*

Think about a personal circumstance in which you felt compelled to lie and later had a miserable time trying to extricate yourself. Trace back and try to write about the event. Or perhaps you would prefer to recount the story of someone else's lie that created a real mess. Either way, remember we have all gone through it!

---

* See *Romeo & Juliet: Plainspoken*, by Greta B. Lipson and Susan Lipson, © 1985, Good Apple, Inc., Carthage, Illinois.

GA1513

What's an Atlas?

An atlas is a comprehensive, bound collection of maps, charts, and tables. Invite the school librarian to come into your classroom with an atlas from the library. Ask him or her to show the class how these books are organized. Give everyone in the class a "hands-on" experience with this remarkable reference book. Learn how to locate information.

As we all know, there are some very significant achievements which occur quite by accident! One of these events transpired in 1570 because of a merchant who lived in Antwerp, Holland. His name was Hooftman and he loved to collect maps and charts. His collection gave him a great deal of pleasure, but he had to constantly roll and unroll the maps. It was a real nuisance and was becoming very time-consuming. As a matter of fact, he was so irritated by the chore that it was taking all the pleasure out of his hobby.

In search of a solution he developed a very sensible idea. He knew of an editor and publisher in the same city whose name was Abraham Ortelius. Hooftman reasoned that a person in the book business could put the seventy maps together into a bound volume. He went to the publisher with this problem and Ortelius readily agreed to organize everything as a book.

The merchant was thrilled with the book and the publisher thought it was an idea that had great commercial promise. Indeed it met with enormous success and Ortelius named the book *Theater of the World*.

This was followed by the work of a cartographer, Gerardus Mercator, who was a world-class mapmaker and who subsequently published a three-volume book of maps. In this way the concept of a world atlas came to be and now can be found in every library.

GA1513

Question for Your Librarian:

From the year 1990 to 1992, the world atlas listed 14,000 name changes and 20 new countries. If this is an example of world change, what are the implications for the study of geography in school? How do cartographers keep current?

After some instruction on the organization and use of the atlas, find your own city in the atlas. How much information does it reveal to you about where you live?

Who Was Atlas?

In classical Greek mythology, Atlas was one of the giant Titans who rebelled against the gods in a battle for power. When the Titans lost, the great god Zeus decreed that Atlas would be severely punished. He was condemned to an eternity of suffering as it was his lifelong burden to hold up the earth and the sky on his shoulders.

Once, Atlas was almost released from his torture by Heracles, who came to ask him for a favor. But Atlas was a fool and because he was outsmarted lost his chance to be freed of his burden. In art, Atlas is seen mostly as a superbly powerful figure supporting the globe.

GA1513

What–Me Worry?

As a class, work up a list on the chalkboard of things that you know kids worry about. These subjects may not be your concerns, but you probably have more insight about your friends and classmates than a lot of adults. How does your list compare to the list of the student in the following poem? Do you believe the last line? Explain.

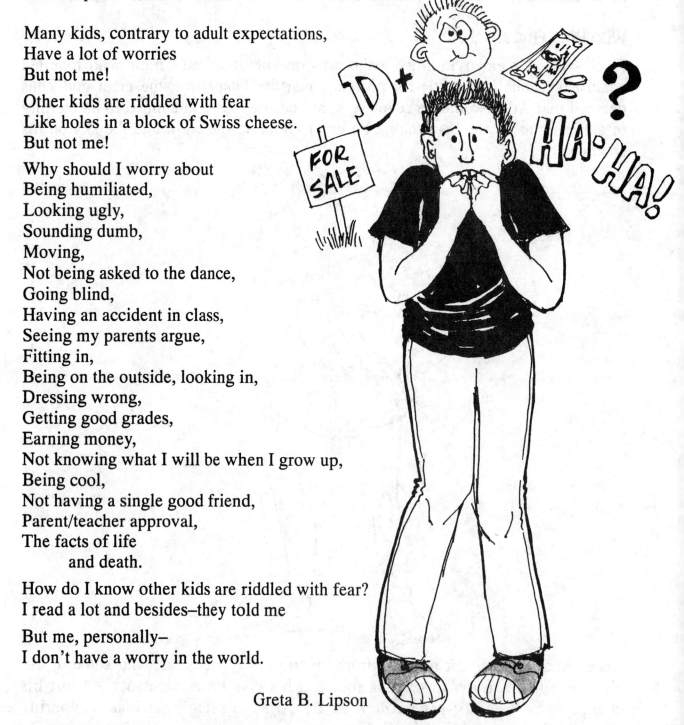

Many kids, contrary to adult expectations,
Have a lot of worries
But not me!

Other kids are riddled with fear
Like holes in a block of Swiss cheese.
But not me!

Why should I worry about
Being humiliated,
Looking ugly,
Sounding dumb,
Moving,
Not being asked to the dance,
Going blind,
Having an accident in class,
Seeing my parents argue,
Fitting in,
Being on the outside, looking in,
Dressing wrong,
Getting good grades,
Earning money,
Not knowing what I will be when I grow up,
Being cool,
Not having a single good friend,
Parent/teacher approval,
The facts of life
        and death.

How do I know other kids are riddled with fear?
I read a lot and besides–they told me

But me, personally–
I don't have a worry in the world.

                          Greta B. Lipson

_____
*_Audacious Poetry_, (GA1417) by Greta B. Lipson, © 1992, Good Apple, Carthage, Illinois.

Whiner's Day

Kevin C. Zaborney is the witty founder of Whiner's Day! It was his insightful idea to establish the day after Christmas as a time of national observance when all the ingrates in the land could complain about the rotten and uninspired gifts they had received for Christmas. We realize that whining is an event which takes place, for some people, all twelve months of the year. It is definitely not limited to December 26!

The whining style deserves some time and analysis since it is unique and unmistakable. Most people recognize the irksome sound which causes the listener's tolerance to "blast off" with exasperation. The whiner's delivery is slow, interminable and is distinguished by its nasality and rhythm. As the whine resonates through the nose, the sound is almost beyond endurance. The refrain of the whine may vary from time to time. Some of the classic themes may be: "That's not fair," "But you promised," "Nobody told me," or "Nobody cares how I feel." Changing the behavior of a whiner is a challenging task. There is no known cure. Whiners have been known to marry one another.

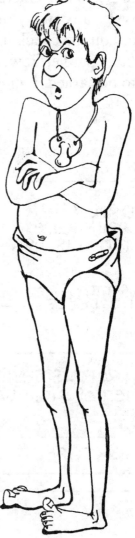

- For scientific purposes, list on the chalkboard all the whining complaints you have ever heard at home and in school.
- When the list is complete have a whiner's contest. Let the volunteers pick a choice from the chalkboard and imitate a whiner.
- Write an account of what you whine about the most. (Come on; admit it.) Justify your behavior in a convincing written paragraph.

GA1513

Write a Check

Did you ever wish that you could whip out your own personal checkbook and write out a cash amount for something you (or some other worthy person) need or want desperately–like they do in the movies? Here is an opportunity to design your own personal check!

Pay particular attention to the information which must be included as in the sample check below. Checks vary in color, printing style, and design. Some may have a logo or insignia, but basically the same information must be included in order for the check to be a legitimate transaction between the "payer" and the "payee." Examine an authentic check, and duplicate the areas of information.

A check is regarded as a legitimate form of financial transaction. It is a written order to a bank to pay the stated amount of money from one's bank account to a designated person or enterprise. You may write out the check for a generous sum of money to anyone you choose. Remember to include all the necessary information on the check including the "memo" which indicates the reason for the check. With a partner, review each other's checks for accuracy. And remember, if a check is to be cashed, it must be endorsed.

CLARK Kenp
THE DAILY PLANET
METROPOLIS, USA

0101

19_____

PAY TO THE ORDER OF _____ $ [   ]

_____ DOLLARS

METROPOLIS SAVINGS BANK
METROPOLIS, USA

FOR _____ _____

⑈:12345б780⑈: 000 123456⑈ 0126

Write a Fan Letter

You would like to know what single book your correspondent read as a young person that had a strong and lasting impact on him or her.

It is always gratifying to write to a celebrity or an important person when you know that you are likely to receive a response to your letter. Good correspondents may be women and men in public office, journalists, business executives, authors of young adult literature, doctors, lawyers, artists, or productive people in all walks of life. A class discussion should help in the decision of whom to write to. Make a list of names with addresses, which may be gathered from reference sources in the library, so that each student can write to a different person.

Since you are interested in more than an autographed picture, your letter must have a message to which others can respond with interest and intelligence. One good idea is to explain at the very beginning that your class is conducting a letter-writing project with an educational objective! At that point you can lead into an inquiry about the most influential book of that person's youth.

Busy people may take a while to answer, but if your class is lucky you may receive some wonderful return letters which can be put on display for the entire school to read. Each student must select a different correspondent so that a variety of letters is ensured.

Yo Jock!

Sports is at the heart and soul of many nations. We talk about sports endlessly and speculate about winners and losers. Winning teams bind people together in the sweetness of victory and the despair of defeat. For a broader view, look into a sports almanac in your library to see just how many games there are in the world. There are many more sporting events than those listed in the word search below.

Archery	Cricket	Hockey	Skating	Swimming
Auto Racing	Curling	Hunting	Skiing	Tennis
Badminton	Fishing	Jogging	Soccer	Track
Baseball	Football	Rugby	Squash	Volleyball
Basketball	Golf	Sailing	Surfing	Wrestling
Bowling				

Word Search

Identify the sports below and circle them. They must be in a straight line, forward, backward, up, down, or diagonal. Do not skip a letter. (Answer key may be found on page 134.) Make your own sports word search on graph paper by adding to the twenty-six events listed.

```
A R C H E R Y L L A B T O O F J
T M A R K C R I C K E T P Q S A
R Q G S T E V E U A Z Q G I A I
A N N R A U T O R A C I N G Y B
C K I U T F L Z L O A N G G B A
K Z L G O L F X I Y E K C O H S
J G T B A D M I N T O N C J D K
O N S Y A S X G G N I H S I F E
G I E H T S O G N I T A K S I T
G F R L Q N E C Z I J D H R S B
I R W U J N B B C X L E U P K A
N U A T E R G G A E E W M I I L
G S A I L I N G W L R N O Q I L
H V V O L L E Y B A L L L B N P
S W I M M I N G H U N T I N G O
```

GA1513

Young Authors' Tea

This lesson would not be complete without a special note of gratitude to Dr. Jack Wayne, the luminous man who always nurtures the creative drive in young people. In his work with pupils or aspiring teachers, his unique vision makes innovation possible. Dr. Wayne, who retired in 1986, is a noble teacher whose kindness, sensitivity, and intelligence are cherished by all. His extraordinary presence is an inspiration to his students, their parents, and a grateful education community.

A very long time ago–in the late 70s–Leona Marla Klein was a student teacher in Dr. Jack Wayne's 6th grade class at Long Elementary in Dearborn, Michigan. Leona and Jack were a magical team–this consummate classroom veteran and his innovative fledgling. One day a famous children's poet, Leland Jacobs, came to the school to speak about the wonders of reading and writing.

Among the many interesting remarks he made was that teachers should invite older students to write for younger children. That was all. Jacobs made no suggestions for strategies nor did he outline a plan of action. But Leona was inspired to carry out her own plan which turned into one of the most successful and exciting projects many veteran teachers had ever seen before or since. Here are the steps in Leona's plan, which was later implemented in a variety of classroom settings (including a class of autistic students).

- First, Leona discussed the plan with the first grade teacher of choice, and together they decided on a date for the proposed Young Authors' Tea.

- Next, she spoke with her sixth graders, each of whom was to be assigned a first grade partner. Their reaction was exuberant!

- A face-to-face meeting was held during which time the big kids were paired off with assigned little partners. The objective was for the older students to discern the interests of their small friends.

- Each older student determined the kinds of subjects his or her first grader liked to read in fiction or nonfiction.

- In their own sessions, the sixth graders discussed fiction, nonfiction, concerns about writing, spelling, and vocabulary, as well as general problems with producing the books.

- Time was set aside for library research and the writing of each book. It took about one hour daily for about three weeks, including group assistance, rewriting, and teacher approval.

- Artists in the classroom illustrated the books which were then bound and completed. Announcements were sent to the first graders inviting them to the Young Authors' Tea.

- The group assembled. The sixth graders read the books to their little partners and then proudly presented them as gifts. Refreshments were served and everyone was the richer for this wonderfully maturing experience.

- Just a reminder that fifth graders, bilingual students, and a variety of other interested students have participated successfully in this project. As always, it is the teacher's call.

Your Future

There is a certain attraction for some people in trying to find out about the future which impels them to consult fortune-tellers, hoping to hear predictions about their lives. Believers in the art of prediction visit a variety of practitioners such as those who read tea leaves or crystal balls, or others who are palm readers and talk about "life lines" or "love lines." Another source of fortune-telling is tarot cards. These are a set of 22 playing cards plus a joker, with each card representing human vices and virtues.

Some who practice the art of foretelling claim to have the power of clairvoyance, which means they have the ability to see objects and events which cannot ordinarily be perceived by the senses. There are mediums and psychics who make claims about having visions of future events, but this is an area which is difficult to prove.

Whatever one believes, it is fun to go to a fair and enter a tent of subdued light where an exotic fortune-teller, in a colorful costume with beads and spangles, offers to tell you which turn your life may take! Even if our futures could be accurately predicted, everyone would not be willing to know what lies ahead. This opens up some interesting questions about the control we may have over our own destiny. Think about the issues on the following page.

 inside label: Your Fortune $5.00

Your Future

Consider This

- If you knew your future, could that future then take place? Explain.
- Would you want to know what is in your future? Does the prospect frighten you, excite you, or make you feel indifferent? Explain your answer.
- We make decisions and choices every day of our lives. How can some choices shape our destiny relative to friends, schoolwork, fun times, romance, or danger?
- Write a paragraph about a single event in your experience which could have changed your life.
- You may also use an episode from history or fiction in which one incident altered the course of events.

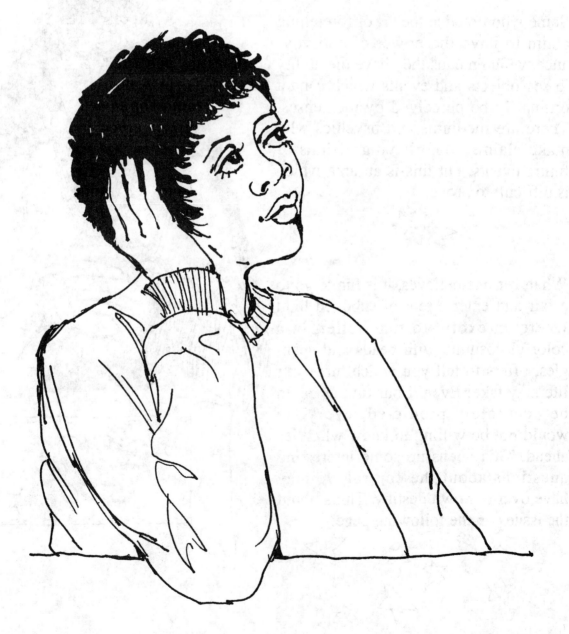

GA1513

5 10 44 75 Your Lucky Number 21 8 16

Numbers are described in *The World Book Encyclopedia* as ideas. The names for number ideas are numerals, which define how many items are in a number. Throughout history, people have given some numbers magical powers or frightening characteristics as in Friday the thirteenth.

Then there is the slang expression "number cruncher," which refers to someone who is very skillful in doing long, complicated calculations. Some people talk about their own lucky numbers which have brought them good luck. So, just for the fun of it you may want to learn how to find your own personal lucky number. There are no guarantees that anything good or magical or lucky will come of your lucky number, but it is fun to work it out.

Make an alphabet chart that looks like the one below. Assign a number to each letter of your name (as indicated on the chart). Add together the numbers of your first name to the numbers of your last name and presto–you have revealed your lucky number.

1	2	3	4	5	6	7	8	9
A	B	C	D	E	F	G	H	I
J	K	L	M	N	O	P	Q	R
S	T	U	V	W	X	Y	Z	

JOSEPH
(1 + 6 + 1 + 5 + 7 + 8)
= 28

ZAKARIA
(8 + 1 + 2 + 1 + 9 + 9 + 1)
= 31

Joseph Zakaria's lucky number is 2831!

GA1513

Zookeeper

Read this sign, which was ordered from a sign company.
A big question follows.

Please do not torment, pester, harass, goad, aggravate, humiliate, mistreat, or hurt the creatures in this place. They must be handled kindly. They sleep and eat just as you do, and sometimes the world does not go well with them. They are ready for you every morning–some, perhaps, more ready than others. If they seem to growl, try to use an understanding tone of voice and they will come around. They are really very nice especially in response to gentle treatment. You may notice that at feeding time they may be somewhat short-tempered. That is because they have been occupied with other things and their stomachs have started to growl. Give them the peace and quiet they need at lunchtime and please leave them alone just as we all prefer to be left alone to take care of our basic needs. They will always do the best they can for you. A smile and a compliment now and then will go a long way. Please respect their responses to the weather, frantic times, and conditions which may affect the finest among us. The person in charge asks only for common courtesy and your cooperation. Remember they get tired, too, and show signs of fatigue! These creatures deserve and thrive on tender, loving care.

The Big Question

What person wrote this and who or what is that person talking about? Someone said it was a zookeeper on behalf of the animals, or an office manager on behalf of the staff. Another said it was a pet store owner or a farmer. Another said it was written by a teacher with a wry sense of humor. Could it be all of these people? Examine the statements. What is your conclusion and how can you support it?

Write a paragraph in which you give your conclusion. Include a topic sentence, supporting details, and a final statement which sums it all up.

132

Suggested Readings

Adler, Irving. *Magic House of Numbers*. New York: John Day Co., 1974.

Espy, Willard R. *An Almanac of Words at Play*. New York: Clarkson N. Potter, Inc., 1975.

Fry, E.B., J.K. Polk, et al., editors. *The Reading Teacher's Book of Lists*. Englewood Cliffs, NJ: Prentice-Hall, Inc., 1984.

Harris, T.L., and R.E. Hodges, editors. *A Dictionary of Reading and Related Terms*. Newark, DE: International Reading Association, 1981.

Hirsch, E.D., Jr., W.G. Rowland, et al., editors. *A First Dictionary of Cultural Literacy*. Boston: Houghton, Mifflin Co., 1989.

Lamb, Geoffrey. *Pencil and Paper Tricks*. Nashville, TN: T. Nelson Publishers, 1977.

Lipson, Greta B. *A Book for All Seasons*. Carthage, IL: Good Apple, Inc., 1990.

Lipson, Greta B. *Audacious Poetry*. Carthage, IL: Good Apple, 1992.

Lipson, Greta B., and Eric B. Lipson. *The Scoop on Frogs and Princes*. Carthage, IL: Good Apple, 1993.

Rogers, James T., editor. *A Dictionary of Cliches*. New York: Facts on File, 1985.

Sebranek, Patrick. *The Write Source Handbook*. Burlington, WI: The Write Source, 1987.

Untermeyer, Louis, editor. *Modern American Poetry*. New York: Harcourt, Brace & Jovanovich, 1962.

Wulffson, Don L. *The Invention of Ordinary Things*. New York: Lothrop, Lee & Shepard, 1981.

Answer Key

Yo Jock! Page 126

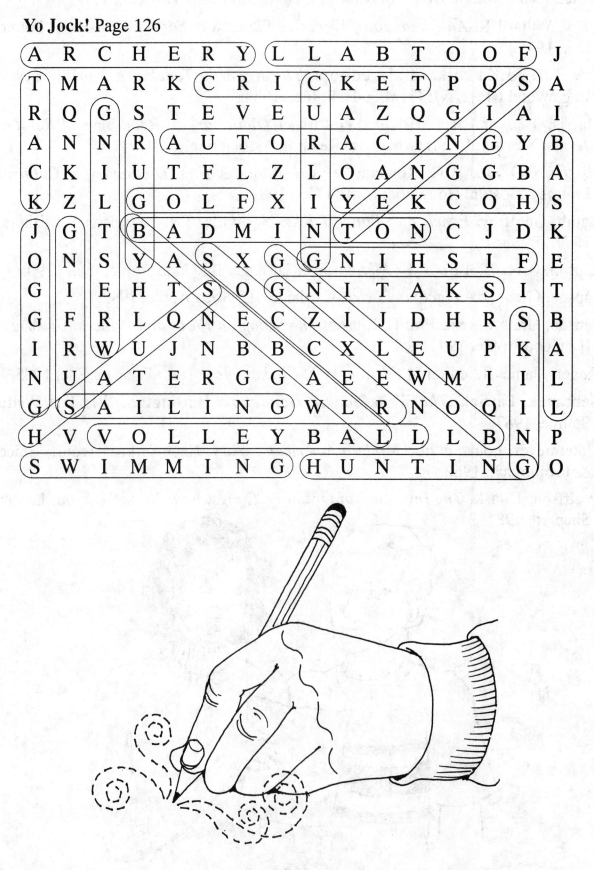

Copyright © 1994, Good Apple

GA1513